D1299823

Research in Business and Marketing

By Murray R. Millson
California State University, Monterey Bay

San Diego, CA

This book is dedicated to our Beagle and my namesake, Murray, who was born on January 10, 2001, and passed away in my arms on February 17, 2011 of cancer. As he sat by our sides or walked with my wife, Joan, and I, he was a constant source of love and strength.

First published in the United States of America in 2011 by Cognella, a division of University Readers, Inc.

15 14 13 12 11   1 2 3 4 5

Printed in the United States of America

ISBN: 978-1-60927-121-3 (hc) / 978-1-5165-1913-2 (br)

Note: The SPSS software used in this book was PASW 18, while the Excel software is Excel 2007

 cognella™

www.cognella.com 800.200.3908

Contents

Introduction

Business is an exciting and exceptionally challenging endeavor from a practitioner's perspective as well as that of academics. Business and its analysis are becoming increasingly more exacting and the ever-increasing computing power that is available puts this powerful analytical muscle at the fingertips of many of us. The use of theory for understanding the relationships among variables is as important now as it has ever been. However, the use of relevant statistics, and standards for measurement and prediction are becoming exceedingly important. Therefore, the definition of a ***Statistic(s)***, as used in this text,

> *is a number or numbers that are derived from samples of data to describe data distributions or test the significance of stated hypotheses.*

The definition of ***Business Statistics***, as used in this text,

> *is a group of methods, processes, and their resulting Statistic(s), that comprise a subset of the vast array of methods, processes, and resulting Statistic(s), that can be employed to describe data distributions or test the significance of stated hypotheses most commonly found in business and marketing situations.*

There are several ways that the study of statistics, the use of statistics, and the meaning of statistics can be pursued. One path of inquiry can be achieved through the study of distributions of data and the derivation of significant metrics that describe those data distributions. While another path for understanding statistics and their use can begin with an analysis of the formulae that result in particular statistics that are associated with various data distributions without particular emphasis on the connections between the distributions and the resulting formulae. In this text, a third path is taken which leads to an understanding of the development, use, and meaning of selected statistics that will be primarily developed though the execution and analysis of SPSS and Excel statistical functions as they relate to a specified dataset.

This text assumes some understanding of various data distributions common to business situations in particular the normal or Gaussian distribution as well as at least a passing familiarity with the formulae that can be used to calculate various statistics often discussed in an Introductory Business Statistics Course. This text also briefly discusses some of the methods that can be used to perform the research process that provides the sample data distributions from which the Statistics are derived. Finally, this text provides detailed paths to follow that result in specific Statistics which can be used to make business and/or marketing decisions.

Chapter 1

Gathering, Measuring, and Describing Data

A. Research and Research Designs

Before we can analyze or gather data, we need to structure a research design. The effective development of a research design requires the researcher to have a fully developed problem statement, opportunity, or knowledge gap that needs to be filled. The development of a problem statement or the identification of an opportunity or a knowledge gap can provide a researcher with preliminary information regarding important concepts and relationships that need attention. Solid problem, opportunity, or knowledge gap development provides significant research direction. To continue the research process, the researcher needs to develop *Research Questions* and *Research Objectives*. Research questions form high level inquiries into the research area of interest which will guide the researcher to more fully developed questions that might be incorporated into a survey instrument or form the basis for an experiment. Research objectives describe in general the outputs or results of a research process. Therefore, research objectives can be thought of as the results of understanding the answers to the research questions. To answer research questions that lead to desired research objectives, researchers need to set the stage to gather data that will lead to information when it is analyzed. Most often it is necessary for researchers to develop a theory or a scenario of how concepts in the problem or opportunity areas of interest are interrelated. Therefore, the basis of all research and its design needs to stem from *theory*.

Theory is often thought to be the depiction in a pictorial or linguistical manner of a particular arrangement of concepts. Theories can be *general statements* developed from evidence, facts, laws, and/or predictions or they can be *general statements* that have been tested to some degree and are thought to be extensively accepted. Hypotheses on the other hand are most often specifically constructed statements that relate concepts in a particular manner. Hypotheses are developed to test portions or entire theories and can be thought of as educated guesses or questions which are structured as statements. Hypotheses and theories cannot be proven (Retrieved from http://plato.stanford.edu/entries/popper/ January 2, 2011). They can only be disproven and then only when based on a predetermined probability. Such probabilities are in general arbitrarily set to accommodate a researcher's level of risk of failure. In the following paragraphs, three well-known research design types will be presented which include *Exploratory Research*, *Descriptive Research*, and *Causal Research*.

Exploratory Research

To get to the point where researchers can develop and/or test a theory or hypothesis, they need to gather the evidence, arguments, and/or facts about selected concepts and their relationships. These facts, arguments, and/or evidence can be gathered from a particular type of research called *Exploratory Research*. Exploratory research can be thought of as a fact-finding mission during which researchers either gather information to perform additional *Descriptive* or *Causal Research*, or use the results of exploratory research as an end product to provide an initial understanding of a concept, of relationships among concepts, or to provide a rudimentary depiction of a research situation or environment. In other words, exploratory research is especially suited for elementary theory building and evidence discovery. In essence all research is exploratory. However, when little knowledge or understanding of a particular area is known, the title of exploratory research is especially applicable.

Exploratory research can be performed through *primary research* or *secondary research*. Primary research is the act of performing research in which the data is derived directly from the original source of the data and is gathered for the purpose of the current research being performed. Secondary research is performed by utilizing and/or investigating others' research output and their perspectives of the data that was derived directly from the original source of the data. Therefore, researchers that use secondary research typically do not perform statistical techniques on such data although it is not incorrect or improper to do so. For example, there is a statistical process known as Meta-Analysis that employs the results of others' quantitative analyses as the data for its analytical processes.

A wide array of techniques can be utilized to perform exploratory research. These techniques are often considered to be a part of the *Qualitative Research* paradigm (Retrieved from http://www.socialresearchmethods.net/kb/qual.php January 2, 2011). The qualitative research paradigm is focused on important issues that include generating theories and hypotheses, achieving a deep understanding of concepts, relationships, and/or situations, and pursuing studies that typically offer a lower level of generalizability than quantitative research methods. These techniques most often employ small sample sizes which will be discussed later in this volume. Five major exploratory/qualitative techniques are presented here with brief descriptions.

- Participant Observation – This technique is also called *Ethnographic Research* and requires the researcher to be immersed in a particular community or environment while simultaneously performing the roles of researcher and community/group member. This technique is appropriate to investigate attitudes, feelings, and opinions as well as behaviors of respondents. Margaret Mead's research portrayed in her book *Coming of Age in Samoa* is an example of this technique.
- Direct Observation – This technique differs from Participant Observation primarily from the perspective of the researcher's detachment from the community or environment under

investigation. This technique, therefore, allows the use of mechanical observation devices such as cameras in addition to human observation. This technique is appropriate to investigate behaviors of respondents. An example of this technique is a toy manufacturer's use of humans and/or video cameras to understand how children respond to new toys.

- Unstructured Interviewing – This technique is an open-ended questioning technique in which initial guiding questions based on the researcher's design and research questions are employed with several follow-up questions to further probe the thoughts and ideas of respondents. This technique is appropriate to primarily investigate attitudes, feelings, and opinions of respondents. An example of this process includes interviewing consumers of household products to determine exactly how a particular product in used in the respondent's home.
- Document Review – This is a process that is also employed in *Historical Research* in which researchers perform primary research by *examining original documents*. This is primary rather than secondary research. This technique is appropriate to investigate stated opinions of and facts about respondents or topics being investigated. Analyzing the United States Declaration of Independence is an example.
- Focus Groups – These research data sources are typically formed from six to twelve participants that are homogeneous in nature. The primary reason for homogeneous respondents is to attempt to reduce the talk or debate regarding issues that are not germane to the primary research question. However, it would be best for the participants to be able to bring forth differing perspectives of the product or issue that forms the essence of the research question. These groups can meet in a face-to-face environment or in an online environment. It is extremely important that there is a facilitator present who is intimately familiar with the particular meeting environment, the important research questions and issues, the challenges of facilitating discussion groups and keeping the members of the focus group on track without stifling discussion, and the ability to summarize the salient outcomes of a focus group session. This technique is appropriate to investigate attitudes, feelings, and opinions of respondents. An example of the use of the focus group technique is to bring ten participants from across the state of California in an online forum to discuss the pros and cons associated with the use of heated seats in new vehicles.

Descriptive Research

Descriptive research is best to gather data that attempts to answer questions regarding *who, what, where, when, and how* factual information associated with particular concepts, situations, and environments but **not** to investigate relationships among concepts or research subjects. Descriptive research *describes* the distribution of data. There are three important measures of distributions that include a distribution's *central tendency*, its *variability* or *dispersion*, and its *shape*.

There are a variety of statistics such as the *mean, median,* and *mode* of a distribution that can be used to provide the bases for such distribution descriptions. The three previously mentioned statistics (*mean, median, and mode*) are used to indicate the *central tendency* of particular types of data distributions that will be discussed shortly. The mean is the arithmetic average of a series of numbers. The median is the middle number in a series of numbers sorted from smallest to largest or largest to smallest. And, the mode of a series of numbers is the number that is found in the greatest frequency in a series of numbers. Additional information may be found at the following web site (Retrieved from http://www.regentsprep.org/regents/math/algebra/AD2/measure.htm January 2, 2011).

A distribution's *variance, standard deviation, range, minimum*, and *maximum* are used to describe it variability or dispersion. The *maximum* number in a series of numbers is the largest number in the series of numbers. The *minimum* number in a series of numbers is the smallest number in the series of numbers. The *range* of a series of numbers is the difference between the maximum and minimum numbers in the series of numbers. The following web site portrays the formulae for the standard deviation and variance of a series of numbers (Retrieved from http://stattrek.com/Lesson3/Variability.aspx January 2, 2011). It can be noted the variance of a series of numbers is the square of the standard deviation of the series of numbers.

Skewness and *kurtosis* are employed to assess the shape of a data distribution. The skewness measure provides an indication of the amount and direction of departure from a normal distribution. The long tail represents the side of the distribution to which it is skewed if skew exists. Positive skew exists when the long tail is associated with larger numbers. Negative skewness exists when the long tail is associated with smaller numbers. Kurtosis provides an indication of the peakedness of a distribution. If a distribution is peaked, it called *leptokurtic* and the kurtosis has a positive value. If a distribution is *not* peaked or it exhibits a *table topped* distribution, it called *platykurtic* and the kurtosis has a negative value. Zero values for skewness and kurtosis suggest that a distribution is close to being normally distributed. The following web site provides further insight into skewness and kurtosis metrics (Retrieved from http://www.spcforexcel.com/are-skewness-and-kurtosis-useful-statistics January 2, 2011).

Causal Research

Causal research is used when the objective is to determine whether one concept or variable causes another concept or variable to change or react. A variable (or variables) that cause or impact another concept or variable is called an *independent* concept(s) or variable (s). Additionally, the concept or variable that is changed or modified as the result of a change in the independent concept or variable is called a *dependent* concept or variable. Managers often consider whether to perform a business activity to achieve desired results. In situations such as these, managers are contemplating causal relationships. A managerial question that exemplifies such a situation is how much might sales increase if prices are decreased by 10%?

An example of the relationships between independent and dependent concepts follows.

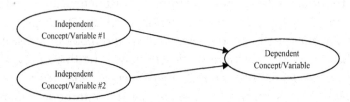

To this point, terms such as concept, variable, etc. have been used interchangeably. In fact they are different. A *concept* can be thought of as any mental image most often of physically tangible items. Many concepts that are studied are much more intangible and difficult to mentally visualize or measure. Such concepts are often called *constructs* since to measure such concepts it is necessary to develop multidimensional measurement instrument scales. For example, whereas a person's weight can be measured with a single metric in pounds, the measurement of a person's satisfaction with a new automobile might necessitate several dimensions or factors. The thought or concept of satisfaction is therefore called a construct. In the previous example, a person's weight in pounds would be considered a variable. *Variables* are considered operationalizations of concepts or constructs. Therefore, the variable satisfaction could be a numerical, aggregated measure of various factors or dimensions that are considered the basis for customer satisfaction with a new automobile. The operationalization of concepts and constructs allow them to be included in mathematical equations and statistical processes. It must be noted that researchers often operationalize constructs with what is known as single element, factor, or dimension measures. An example of this situation would be when a researcher asks a respondent to provide his or her satisfaction with a new automobile by selecting a single number from one to five with five being very satisfied and one being very unsatisfied.

Causal relationships can be characterized by three major constraints that include (1) high correlations between and among dependent and independent variables or factors, (2) the timing of changes in independent concepts or variables must occur prior to changes in dependent concepts or variables, and (3) the elimination of all other possible concept or variable changes or modifications that might have caused the effect or result of interest. Using slightly different wording, Cook and Campbell (1979) identify three key criteria for inferring a cause and effect relationship: (a) covariation between the presumed cause(s) and effect(s); (b) temporal precedence of the cause(s); and (c) exclusion of alternative explanations for cause-effect linkages.

To effectively investigate causal relationships, researchers need to eliminate several confounding forces or contaminants to understanding the valid structure of causal relationships. There are a variety of measures of *validity*. A major variety of validity can be stated as *measuring or assessing what you believe you are measuring or assessing*. This type of validity is called *construct validity*. Another validity variety important to causal relationships is *internal validity*. Internal validity suggests the relationship(s) between two or more concepts, constructs, or variables truly exist. *Experimental designs* are the most effective mechanism for assessing and controlling internal validity. An example of internal validity can be understood by considering the following scenario. If a researcher develops a study to measure the relationship between the degree of customers' intentions to purchase particular products then the researcher's study is valid if the research process accurately measures how much customers' purchase behaviors changes when the customers' purchase intentions change.

Six important experimental design confounding contaminants or threats to internal validity include:

1. Selection of study subjects.
2. History (*events which occur between observations or measurements*) as a threat to internal validity.

3. Maturation (*emotional, psychological, or physiological processes that impact study subjects over time*) as a threat to internal validity.
4. Mortality (*loss of study subjects from research groups*) as a threat to internal validity.
5. Instrumentation which suggests that observers or measuring instruments might exhibit fluctuations that might impact experimental outcomes.
6. Testing which suggests that a pretest might add to or influence a post test.

There are methods by which the previous confounding contaminants or threats to internal validity can be eliminated or mitigated.

1. Obtain *random samples* of respondents from the entire group of subjects being studied and *randomly assign* the randomly selected subjects to study groups.
2. History can be removed as a threat to internal validity by assuring that there are multiple experimental groups and they all experience the same experiences except for the experimental treatment.
3. Maturation can be removed as a threat to internal validity by assuring that the same amount of time passes for each subject/respondent in an experiment.
4. Mortality can be removed as a threat to internal validity by performing both pre and post tests on multiple study groups.
5. Instrumentation problems can be eliminated or mitigated by assuring mechanical/electrical instruments are calibrated and/or observers are trained.
6. Testing can be eliminated or mitigated by also incorporating Treatment and Control groups that do not receive pre-tests.

There are a variety of experimental designs that can be used to study cause and effect relationships. The most effective at eliminating or mitigating threats to internal validity is the *Solomon Four Group Design*. However, this design requires several study subjects that need to be randomly assigned to four study groups. Two of the experimental groups are called *treatment* groups whereas the other two experimental groups are called *control* groups. The treatment groups are provided a different experience than the control group. That experience is the basis for the experiment in that the experiment is to assess the differential responses of the groups that receive a treatment from the groups that do not receive a treatment. The first treatment group is provided a test or observation (pre-test) prior to a treatment as well as a test or observation (post test) after a treatment whereas the second treatment group is provided a treatment and a test or observation (post test) after the treatment at the same time as the first treatment group but no test or observation prior to the treatment (pre-test). The first control group is provided a test or observation (pre-test) at the same time as the first treatment group and a test or observation (post test) at the same time as the first treatment group but no treatment is provided to this control group between the two tests or observations. The second control group is only provided a test or observation (post test) at the same time as all of the other study groups. Each of these groups is provided pre-tests and post tests. Treatments are indicated by the Xs in the boxes below. The following depicts the Solomon Four Group Design. Other experimental designs can be used to save time and money by employing

Treatment Group #1 and Control Group #1noted below however the use of this model opens the experiment to threats to internal validity.

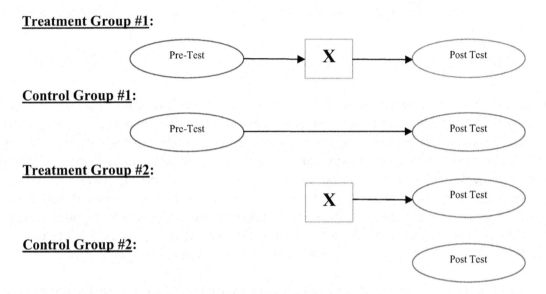

Treatment Group #1:

Pre-Test → X → Post Test

Control Group #1:

Pre-Test → Post Test

Treatment Group #2:

X → Post Test

Control Group #2:

Post Test

B. Data Types and Survey Questions

To perform any research, researchers need data. There are *four major types of data* discussed below that include *nominal/categorical, ordinal, interval, and ratio.*

1. *Nominal/Categorical* data are data depicted by subject information that can only be described by grouping subjects with similar characteristics. For example, gender should be measured as nominal/categorical data. Gender is measured by counting respondents that are representative of two groups of subjects which comprise males and females.
2. *Ordinal* data is a higher order of data than nominal/categorical data since ordinal data provides additional information above that of subject classification. Ordinal data provides information regarding the relative position among subjects which allows subjects to be ordered according to at least one of the subjects' common attributes. Ordinal data does not require any particular distance between subjects to demonstrate the ordering of subjects.
3. *Interval* data is data that can provide a greater degree of information than ordinal data. Interval data demonstrates the ordering of subjects according to at least one common attribute however interval data is also defined by data that demonstrates equidistant spacing between data points.
4. *Ratio* data is data that is characterized by the property of having a zero point in the data. Due to this attribute, ratio data can be multiplied and divided to form percentages and ratios.

It is important to note that ALL higher order types of data can be collapsed to form data types at lower levels for example ALL data types can be collapsed into groups to form nominal/categorical data. Ratio and Interval data are often called scaled data or quantitative data since these data are most often gathered using survey instrument scales. Moreover, ratio and interval data is called parametric data and can be analyzed using parametric statistical techniques whereas ordinal and nominal/categorical data are called non-parametric data and requires non-parametric statistical techniques to analyze. These data can also be usefully presented using histograms and other graphical methods.

Survey Questions

A variety of survey questions can be used to obtain the appropriate data to be able to employ the proper statistical techniques to derive the necessary information to make the needed managerial decisions that lead to the objectives of a research process. Prior to presenting questions, it is important to provide a brief introduction that includes the identity of the organization offering the survey, the purpose of the survey, confirmation of information confidentiality or anonymity, the approximate amount of time necessary to complete the survey instrument, and how the information will be used. If this introductory information might bias respondents' survey instrument responses, some of these items may need to be modified. In most instances, it is a good practice to debrief respondents after the data has been gathered and the analyses have been performed.

1. Survey instruments are most often structured such that the questions that are first encountered by a respondent qualify the respondent to participate in the survey process. Such a question might ask if the respondent has used a shampoo within the past two weeks. If the respondent has, he or she would be allowed to continue. If he or she has not, the respondent should be thanked and asked to end the survey process.
2. After the respondent is presented qualifying questions, he or she encounters questions that are important to the survey process but are not threatening, do not require significant memory or recall, nor are they difficult to answer. These questions should also be intriguing to respondents to capture their interest.
3. The next group or groups of questions should be structured in a clear orderly manner. They can be ordered by topic, chronologically, or some other clear sequence. These questions comprise the heart of the information needed.
4. If the survey instrument contains groups of questions, there should be brief transitional information between groups to hold the respondent's interest and make sure that the respondent understands the content of each group or section, and what lies ahead.
5. If the survey instrument contains sensitive questions that are germane to the research questions, they can be included next. Respondents should feel comfortable with the survey topic, the importance of the topic's purpose, and the identified survey provider at this point in the survey process. This provides the greatest likelihood of receiving valid information regarding these questions.
6. Finally, most research needs to gather demographic data that is typically nominal/categorical in nature. Such demographic data can be used to understand how different groups of

respondents relate to the important information being gathered in addition to provide a profile of the survey's respondents.

Nominal/Categorical Survey Question Examples [Screening or Demographic Questions]

1. Have you purchased **Soapy** shampoo in the past two weeks?
   Yes   ☐ No☐
2. What is your age category in years?
   20-39 ☐ 40-59 ☐ 60-79☐

Ordinal Survey Instrument Question Examples [Preference, Time Sequence, etc.]

1. Indicate your preference for the following drinks by inserting a 1 for the most preferred through 3 for the least preferred.
   Soda ☐
   Water ☐
   Juice ☐
2. Indicate which came first in your life by inserting a 1 for the earliest through 3 for the latest.
   Started working ☐
   Got married ☐
   Graduated from high school ☐

Interval Survey Instrument Question Examples [Measure the degree of something]

1. I am completely satisfied with **Soapy** shampoo. [7 point scale-center point undecided]
   Strongly Agree ___ ___ ___ ___ ___ ___ ___ Strongly Disagree
2. I intend to purchase **Soapy** shampoo in the next two weeks. [6 point scale-no undecided point]
   Strongly Agree ___ ___ ___ ___ ___ ___ Strongly Disagree

Ratio Survey Instrument Question Examples [Provides ability to compare relative measures]

1. What is your age?   _____
2. What is your height in feet?   _____

C. Populations, Samples, and Sampling

A *population* is defined as a group of ALL of the potential subjects a researcher is attempting to study. For example, a researcher might define a population as ALL women in the United States, or North America, or China. For sampling purposes, populations are typically represented by *sampling frames*. Therefore, sampling frames are surrogate lists of subjects of people or organizations that can be used to create samples of the appropriate subjects. For example, a researcher might use a list of registered voters in a city or area to represent the researcher's population of interest. Of course, depending on the subject of the research, a voter registration list may cause significant sampling frame error especially if the research question of the study is *what makes people not register to vote*.

A *census* is an enumeration and study of ALL of the subjects in a population. Typically a census is not possible due to access of the subjects or financial concerns or, if it is possible, and those concerns are circumvented, a wide variety of what are called non-sampling errors can occur. *Sampling errors* are due exclusively to drawing probability samples as opposed to conducting a complete enumeration of a population whereas *non-sampling errors* are associated primarily with data gathering and processing procedures. The following are *non-sampling errors* that are prevalent in the performance of census activities as well as research that is performed through the use of sampling processes.

1. Sampling frame errors which occur when the sampling frame used by researchers is out of alignment with the population of interest.
2. Data specification errors which come from not determining exactly what type of data is needed to perform the desired analyses.
3. Inappropriate data gathering methods and processes for example using survey techniques when observation techniques are more appropriate and employing open-ended survey instrument questions rather than closed-ended questions or scaled questions.
4. Omission of necessary data which occurs when researchers do not include the proper questions in interviews and/or survey instruments.
5. Errors due to untrained field workers who either unintentionally or intentionally make mistakes that lead to erroneous data collection.
6. Errors derived from coding, transcribing, and manipulating data after the data has been provided by respondents.
7. Mistakes in presenting and reporting data analyses and results.
8. Machines used in data processing can also lead to errors when their operations are faulty.

All of these non-sampling errors are under the control of researchers. Therefore, such errors can be mitigated but it is most difficult to eliminate them altogether. Good attention to detail, and research quality control procedures and processes can help reduce non-sampling errors and their detrimental impact.

Probability Samples

Simple Random Sampling

The sampling process of *Simple Random Sampling* attempts to assure that each member of a population/sampling frame has an equal probability of being selected as a member of the sample. That probability can be calculated as [1 / number of subjects in the population or sampling frame].

The randomness of a sample provides a research study with a representativeness of the population. There is no other way to assure sample *representativeness* than a random sampling of the population or sampling frame. A common misconception is that the larger the sample, the greater its representativeness will be. This is not true. However, the greater the sample size, the greater the *accuracy* of the statistics generated by the research. But, the research accuracy versus sample size relationship is not linear. In fact, after sample sizes reach 1,000 to 2,000 subjects, research accuracy increases very little. The following graph was developed using a worst case standard deviation of 1.3 from a 7-point Likert scale and a z of 1.96 representing a 95% confidence interval. A researcher must recognize that there is a tradeoff between the cost of research and the value and reliability of the information obtained from research.

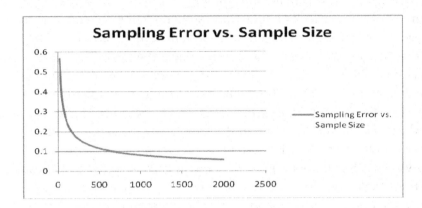

There are two ways to select simple random samples. The first method is *simple random sampling with replacement*. This method provides an equal probability for each population subject to be selected since the first sample subject is selected with a probability of [1 / the number of subjects in the population] and then *replaced* in the population/sampling frame so that the number in the population/sampling remains constant. However, the use of such an approach allows a particular population/sampling frame subject to be selected more than once. The second manner by which simple random samples can be selected is called *simple random sampling without replacement*. This process suggests that subjects that are selected from the population/sampling frame are not replaced prior to the selection of ensuing sample members. This process solves the problem of selecting the same population/sampling frame subject more than once for sample membership however as sample subjects are selected the probability of each ensuing sample member is increased. In both of these approaches, the *unit of analysis* is an individual subject listed in the population/sampling frame. For example, the probability of selecting the second sample member from a population/sampling frame with N subjects is [1 / (number of subjects in the population/sampling frame - 1)]. One is subtracted from the number of subjects in the population/sampling frame because the initial sample member taken from the population/sampling frame is not replaced for potential future selection. It can be seen that *Simple Random Sampling* provides random samples however this process necessitates an itemized, ordered list of the population or sampling frame which can be difficult to obtain in many instances.

Noted below is a version of a random number table. Each number (0 through 9) in a random number table can be generated using a 10 sided die or computer software. A researcher can select a sample from a *numerically ordered population/sampling frame* by choosing a random starting point in the random number table and traversing the random number table in any of four directions (up-down-left-right) from the starting point. The researcher can close his or her eyes and point to the random number table to provide a random starting number. The *size* of each number to be selected must be equivalent to the number of digits in the population/sampling frame. For example, if the number of subjects in the population/sampling frame is N = 400 subjects and numbered from 001 through 400, then each number to be selected from the random number table to create a sample must be 3 digits long. Using a population/sampling frame size of N = 400, select a sample of n = 4. The random starting point that was created by the researcher in the manner described above is found in the RED ELLIPSE which circles the three digit number 910 (bottom of columns 9, 10, and 11) in the random number table below. The population/sampling frame contains 400 subjects so the number 910 is not a member of this particular population/sampling frame. To continue to select the members of the sample, the researcher can traverse the random number table in any one of four directions. In this instance, the researcher decided to move down the table therefore the next two numbers to be considered are 936 and 636. Neither of these numbers can be found in the population/sampling frame under consideration. The researcher now moves to the top of the next column of three digit numbers which is identified by the BLUE ELLIPSE noted on the random number table and circles 713 which also cannot be found in the stipulated population/sampling frame. Note that the larger spaces between columns in random number tables have no particular significance other than to make viewing the numbers and traversing the table easier. As we move to the next three numbers down the table, we find *190*, 396, and *364*. These three numbers can be found in the list of 400 subjects in the population/sampling frame of interest and become the first

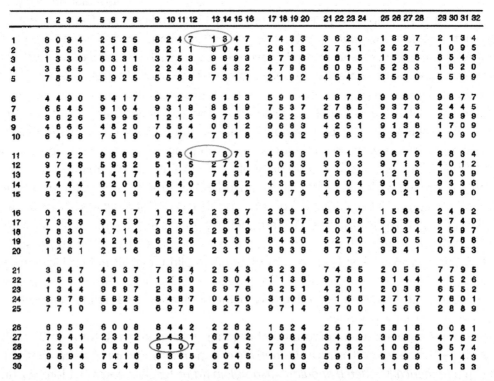

	1 2 3 4	5 6 7 8	9 10 11 12	13 14 15 16	17 18 19 20	21 22 23 24	25 26 27 28	29 30 31 32
1	8 0 9 4	2 5 2 5	8 2 4 7	1 3 4 7	7 4 3 3	3 6 2 0	1 8 9 7	2 1 3 4
2	3 5 6 3	2 1 9 6	8 2 1 1	9 0 4 5	2 6 1 8	2 7 5 1	2 6 2 7	1 0 9 5
3	1 3 3 0	6 3 3 1	3 7 5 3	9 6 9 3	6 7 3 8	6 6 1 5	1 5 3 6	6 5 4 3
4	3 5 6 5	0 0 1 6	2 2 4 3	6 4 3 2	4 7 9 6	6 0 9 5	5 2 8 3	1 6 2 0
5	7 8 5 0	5 9 2 5	5 5 8 8	7 3 1 1	2 1 9 2	4 5 4 5	3 5 3 0	5 5 8 9
6	4 4 9 0	5 4 1 7	9 7 2 7	6 1 5 3	5 9 0 1	4 8 7 8	9 9 8 0	9 8 7 7
7	6 5 4 5	9 1 0 4	9 3 1 8	8 8 1 9	7 5 3 7	2 7 8 5	9 3 7 3	2 4 4 5
8	3 6 2 6	5 9 9 5	1 2 1 5	9 7 5 3	9 2 2 3	5 6 5 8	2 9 4 4	2 8 9 9
9	4 6 6 5	4 8 2 0	7 5 5 4	0 6 1 2	9 6 8 3	4 2 5 1	9 1 3 8	1 7 0 9
10	6 4 9 8	7 5 1 9	0 4 7 4	7 8 1 8	6 8 3 2	9 6 8 3	9 8 7 2	4 0 9 0
11	6 7 2 2	9 8 6 9	9 3 6 1	7 8 7 5	4 8 8 3	1 3 1 5	9 6 7 9	8 8 3 4
12	9 7 4 8	5 9 3 2	5 1 1 5	2 7 2 1	0 0 3 3	9 3 0 3	9 7 1 3	4 0 1 2
13	5 6 4 1	1 4 1 7	1 4 1 9	7 4 3 4	8 1 6 5	7 3 6 8	1 2 1 8	5 0 3 9
14	7 4 4 4	9 2 0 0	8 8 4 0	5 8 8 2	4 3 9 8	3 9 0 4	9 1 9 9	9 3 3 6
15	8 2 7 9	3 0 1 9	4 6 7 2	3 7 4 3	3 9 7 9	4 6 8 9	9 0 2 1	6 9 9 0
16	0 1 6 1	7 6 1 7	1 0 2 4	2 3 8 7	2 8 9 1	6 6 7 7	1 5 8 5	2 4 8 2
17	7 3 8 8	9 7 5 9	7 5 5 5	6 6 2 4	9 9 7 7	2 0 0 8	5 5 9 6	9 7 4 0
18	7 8 3 0	4 7 1 4	3 6 9 5	2 9 1 9	1 8 0 4	4 0 4 4	1 0 3 4	2 5 9 7
19	9 8 8 7	4 2 1 6	6 5 2 6	4 5 3 5	8 4 3 0	5 2 7 0	9 6 0 5	0 7 6 6
20	1 2 6 1	2 5 1 6	8 5 6 9	2 3 1 0	3 9 3 9	8 7 0 3	9 8 4 1	0 3 5 3
21	3 9 4 7	4 9 3 7	7 6 3 4	2 5 4 3	6 2 3 9	7 4 5 5	2 0 5 5	7 7 9 5
22	4 5 5 0	8 1 0 3	1 2 5 0	2 3 0 4	1 1 3 8	9 7 8 8	9 1 4 4	4 5 2 6
23	1 3 4 4	9 6 9 7	2 3 8 3	6 9 7 6	6 2 5 1	4 2 0 1	2 0 3 8	6 5 5 2
24	8 9 7 6	5 8 2 3	8 4 8 7	0 4 6 0	3 1 0 6	9 1 6 6	2 7 1 7	7 6 0 1
25	7 7 1 0	9 9 4 3	6 9 7 8	8 2 7 3	9 7 1 4	9 7 0 0	1 5 6 6	2 8 8 9
26	6 9 5 9	6 0 0 8	8 4 4 2	2 2 8 2	1 5 2 4	2 5 1 7	5 8 1 8	0 0 8 1
27	7 9 4 1	2 3 1 2	2 4 3 1	6 7 0 2	9 9 8 4	3 4 6 9	3 0 8 5	4 7 6 2
28	2 2 8 4	0 8 9 6	9 1 0 7	5 5 4 2	7 3 1 9	3 7 8 2	1 0 6 8	9 5 7 4
29	9 5 9 4	7 4 1 6	9 3 6 5	6 0 4 6	1 1 8 3	5 9 1 6	9 5 9 9	1 1 4 3
30	4 6 1 3	6 5 4 9	6 3 6 9	3 2 0 8	5 1 0 9	9 6 8 0	1 1 6 8	6 1 3 3

Retrieved from http://apps.who.int/medicinedocs/fr/d/Jwhozip14e/9.html January 7, 2011.

three sample members of the required sample of four. As the researcher moves down the table, the fourth and final sample subject member is not located in the table until the number *178* is encountered. The final simple random sample of four taken from the ordered population/sampling frame of 400 in this case includes the numbers 190, 396, 364, and 178. It should be noted that there is no significance in the order by which the sample numbers are drawn.

Systematic Random Sampling

Systematic Random Sampling is another method to draw or create a random sample that can be developed with or without a physical, itemized, ordered sampling frame. When *Systematic Random Sampling* is employed, the *unit of analysis* is an individual subject listed in the population/sampling frame or stream of potential sample subjects as described below.

The use of *Systematic Random Sampling* with a physical, itemized, ordered sampling frame does not require the use of a random number table as noted above. The random starting point is set as a number in the population/sampling frame list between and including 1 and an increment value k. The value of k can be calculated by dividing the population/sampling frame size by the desired sample size. Therefore, the randomness of the sample is derived from the random starting point in the population/sampling frame list and selecting every k^{th} subject in the list after the random starting point. This provides equal spacing between the choices of sample subjects after the initial random selection of the first sample member. For example, if the population/sampling frame was N = 300 subjects in length, a sample size of n = 6 subjects was desired, and a random starting point was determined from a random number table to be 15, then the sample would be formed by selecting the 15th subject in the population/sampling frame and every k^{th} [k = N/n = 300/6 = 50] after that. Therefore, the six sample subjects would be those subjects represented by the numbers 15, 65, 115, 165, 215, and 265.

A second approach for employing *Systematic Random Sampling* that does not require the use of a physical, itemized, ordered sampling frame involves the creation of a sample from a stream of subjects such as individuals leaving or entering a shopping mall or store. The sampling process is quite similar to that described above. However a sampling start time and end time are important as is an assessment of the number of subjects that will be passing the sampling point. The number of subjects that will be passing the sampling point during the sampling period can be considered the population or sampling frame. For example, a researcher might consider people who shop at a particular store on Monday's in the afternoon to form a particular population from which a sample might be taken. To develop such a sample, the researcher would determine approximately how many people will pass the sampling point during the afternoon time period. That number can be considered N or the population. As demonstrated earlier, the researcher must determine the sample size (n). From the sample size and the population estimate, the researcher can calculate k. For example, assume that the population is estimated to comprise N = 200 potential shoppers passing the sampling point during the sampling time period and a sample size of n = 5 is desired. The researcher can now calculate k to be 40 using the following formula [k = N/n = 200/5 = 40]. Also, as noted above, the random starting point needs to be between 1 and k or in this instance 1 and 40 inclusive. Therefore, if the researcher determines the random starting point from a random number table to be 25, the five sample subjects would be those subjects represented by the numbers 25, 65, 105, 145, and 185.

Unlike *Simple Random Sampling*, *Systematic Random Sampling* provides random samples however this process does not always necessitate an itemized, ordered list of the population or sampling frame. Therefore, *Systematic Random Sampling* is a good choice to create a random sample when sampling frames that represent the population of interest are not available. Researchers must be careful, when using *Systematic Random Sampling* as described in the second instance, to precisely define the populations being investigated. As noted in the store shopping example above, the sample created in that example *is not necessarily a sample of ALL shoppers of that particular store, of all of its franchised branches, or of ALL of the exit doors of the store.*

Cluster Sampling

Cluster Sampling is a sampling process that can be executed in a couple of different ways. Cluster sampling can be executed as a one or two stage cluster sampling process. To perform *One Stage Cluster Sampling*, a researcher often needs to have a population of subjects that are or can be grouped into defined clusters or groups. It is assumed that such groups are of equal size in terms of units of analysis. A cluster sample can involve households in a city or region. In this scenario, the *unit of analysis* in the study is a household. A city can be divided by city blocks or a region might be divided by municipal districts. For example, a researcher might identify all of the city blocks by numbering them. A random number table can be used to select a random sample out of the population of city blocks. Therefore, each city block would have an equal probability to be represented in the sample. The population of city blocks would be N and the number of blocks in the sample would be n. The probability of a city block being selected for the sample is [n / N]. This sampling process requires the researcher to interview and/or survey EVERY household in the city blocks selected as members of the sample.

Another way to perform *Cluster Sampling* is called *Two Stage Cluster Sampling*. The *Two Stage Cluster Sampling* process begins as did the *One Stage Cluster Sampling* process with a random selection of a set of groups from a population of groups. As noted, the *One Stage Cluster Sampling* process requires sampling ALL of the units of analysis (households) in the city blocks selected in the sample of city blocks. In the *Two Stage Cluster Sampling* process, there is an additional random selection process. After the sample of city blocks is randomly selected, a random selection of households from each selected city block is also selected. This means that the researcher needs itemized lists of the subjects contained within each of the groups (city blocks in this example) selected in the *One Stage Cluster Sampling* process. The final sample consists of randomly selected households within a set of randomly selected city blocks. Therefore, the random selection of subjects from a randomly selected set of grouping subjects is a random selection of subjects. One or Two Stage Cluster Sampling processes do not need lists or sampling frames to select samples to represent populations however One or Two Stage Cluster Sampling processes do require lists or sampling frames to select samples to represent populations when the initial groups or blocks and/or the final number of items/members within groups/blocks is large.

Stratified Sampling

Stratified Sampling is another sampling technique in which the researcher can identify groups of subjects in a population. Unlike *Cluster Sampling, Stratified Sampling* is most often concerned with populations that are formed by groups with unequal sizes. Therefore, *Stratified Sampling* can effectively create samples and assist the analysis of data from populations containing groups of varying sizes some of which are significantly small groups of subjects. The process by which *Stratified Sampling* is executed is to identify the various groups within a population of interest. Next, the researcher needs an itemization of the subjects within each of the groups or stratum within the population. Whereas *Cluster Sampling* focuses on groups that are relatively similar in size, *Stratified Sampling* is effectively used with study groups or subpopulations that are different sizes. To employ *Stratified Sampling* it is also assumed that there is homogeneity of subjects within each stratum. To complete the development of a *Stratified Sampling* process, the researcher takes a simple random sample from each stratum with sample sizes that are proportional to the sizes of the population within each stratum. Once statistics such as means of measured variables from each stratum are calculated, overall statistics such as means can be calculated by weighting the means of the various strata by the ratio of the size of each stratum to the overall population size. For a *Stratified Sampling* example comprising two strata, the weighted sample mean can be calculated by [Weighted Sample Mean = [mean1 (stratum1 size/population size)] + [mean2 (stratum2 size/population size)].

Non-Probability Samples

Non-Probability Samples are often employed when sampling frames are not readily available, when experts or key informants may have insight that general population respondents do not have, when a pilot study is needed to test a survey instrument, when probability sampling techniques are too expensive to perform, or when the unit of analysis is elusive in the population and/or exceptionally small in number in the population. Since non-probability samples are not necessarily representative of the population of interest, the sample size does not suggest much about the confidence interval of the statistics being considered. Therefore, the size of the sample does not have a great deal of relevance. It can however impact the analysis of the data since sample size influences the degrees of freedom which are important in the location process of specific tabled statistics such as *t* and *F* statistics.

Convenience Sampling

Convenience Sampling appears to be the most commonly used non-probability sampling technique. It is often used since it employs subjects that are *convenient* to the researcher. This technique can provide valid information however there is no excellent way to assure such validity. The process of *Convenience Sampling* involves the surveying of units of analysis such as people who are convenient to researchers such as students in a classroom, colleagues in an office environment, people walking down a street, or any other group or stream of people in a public or private venue.

Quota Sampling

Quota Sampling suggests that specified numbers of various groups of units of analysis are employed in a research project. Often *Quota Sampling* assures that equal numbers of men and women are included in a sample however equal numbers of employed and unemployed people might also be used in a *Quota Sampling* process. Additionally, in a university research project *Quota Sampling* might require equal numbers of undergraduate and graduate students or equal numbers of students in each class level (Freshmen, Sophomores, Juniors, and Seniors). *Quota Sampling* is a non-probability surrogate for *Stratified Sampling*. It performs the function of forcing the sample to contain data from various groups of strata in the population of interest but it does not provide the representativeness of the population in the samples from the various strata.

Judgment Sampling/Purposive Sampling/Key Informant Sampling/Expert Sampling

Judgment/Purposive/Key Informant/Expert Sampling can be effectively employed when it is thought that the general population does not have the insight to effectively provide answers to important survey questions. Such a process is executed by determining who the experts or key informants are in a particular field. Next, the researcher interviews or provides a survey instrument to the selected experts or key informants. This process is somewhat similar to *Convenience Sampling* however a researcher needs to have the ability to gain access to the experts or key informants. This can be a significant impediment in a research process.

The similarity of responses by several respondents or raters can be assessed by calculating an Inter-Rater or Inter-Observer reliability score. An Inter-Rater or Inter-Observer reliability score can be determined for both nominal/categorical and continuous (scaled/interval/ratio) data. Nominal/categorical data Inter-Rater or Inter-Observer reliability can be determined by calculating the percent of instances in which all of the raters, judges, or experts provide the same answers. For continuous (scaled/interval/ratio) data Inter-Rater or Inter-Observer reliability, the researcher can calculate a Pearson Product Moment Correlation (this process is addressed in Chapter 3) regarding the scores provided by the raters, judges, or experts.

Snowball Sampling

Snowball Sampling is a specialized sampling technique that can be employed to locate respondents associated with rare and/or specialized information such as people with rare diseases, people with certain disabilities, homeless people, etc. The *Snowball Sampling* process requires the researcher to locate at least one individual (unit of analysis) in the population of interest. The ensuing respondents are located through referrals from and nominations by the initial respondent(s).

D. Sample Size Determination

The sizes of samples depend on a number of factors. To determine the appropriate sample size, a researcher needs to understand what the most important questions are in a survey instrument or what survey instrument question type needs the greatest sample size. A researcher may want to gather data from a sample that minimizes the cost of a survey process while not exceeding a particular level of error. Therefore, the researcher needs to determine the question that is most important to him or her and calculate a sample size using the maximum amount of error allowable. Additionally, questions that yield categorical data require the use of a different equation to calculate a sample size than questions that yield scaled (interval or ratio) data.

A sample size can be calculated based on a categorical/dichotomous question by employing the following formula.

$n = z^2 (p\ q) / e^2$ where n = sample size; z = standard score representing the area under a normal curve; p = percent of an attribute Judgment Sampling/Purposive Sampling/Key Informant Sampling/Expert Sampling present in the population; q = percent of an attribute thought to be not present in the population (1 - p); and e = ± allowable error.

The most conservative sample size is obtained when both p and q are equal to 50%. The sample size based on a dichotomous question such as gender with an allowable error of ±2% and a confidence interval of 95% (z = 1.96) is as follows.

$n = (1.96)^2 (50 \times 50) / 2^2 = 2{,}401$ = the needed sample size.

A sample size can be calculated based on an interval or ratio question by employing the following formula.

$n = (z^2 \times s^2) / e^2$ where n = sample size; z = standard score representing the area under a normal curve; s = population standard deviation; e = ± allowable error.

The most conservative (largest) sample size is obtained when the researcher estimates the standard deviation of the population, if unknown, using the most conservative estimate possible. The most conservative estimate possible of a standard deviation is to consider the maximum range of a continuous variable and divide that range into six standard deviations or 6σ. For example, if a researcher divides a 7-point Likert scale into a maximum 6σ, the resulting standard deviation would be calculated by dividing 7 by 6 = 1.167. For this example, the researcher will use a 95% confidence interval (z = 1.96) and an allowable error of ±0.5 points on a 7-point scale.

$n = [(1.96)^2 \times (1.167)^2] / (0.5)^2 = 20.93 = 21$ = the needed sample size.

E. Sampling Distributions

A *sampling distribution* is a distribution of a statistic, such as means, obtained from numerous samples from a single population. Therefore, every statistic has a sampling distribution. A true sampling distribution can only be created from an infinite number of samples. The mean of such a sampling distribution is, therefore, a mean of means. The true mean of a population is usually unknown, is called a parameter, and is represented by the Greek letter mu (μ) whereas the mean of a single sample can be calculated, is called a statistic, and is represented by ($\bar{x}$). Many sampling

distributions are normal, bell-shaped, or Gaussian. The average of the sample means is the population mean as the number of samples approaches infinity. The standard deviation or variance of a sampling distribution is not well represented by the standard deviation or variance of a single sample. The standard deviation of a single sample is much wider than the standard deviation of a respective sampling distribution. The standard deviation of a sampling distribution is reduced by dividing the sample standard deviation by the square root of the sample size.

F. Data Distributions

The most often encountered data distributions found in business include the Gaussian, Normal, or Bell-Shaped Distribution, the Student *t* Distribution, the Chi Square Distribution, the F Distribution, the Weibull, the Poisson, Logistics or S-Shaped Distribution, and several others. Of chief concern to this text are the Gaussian, Normal, or Bell-Shaped, the Student *t*, the Chi Square, and the F Distributions. Diagrams of these distributions follow.

Gaussian, Normal, or Bell-Shaped Distribution:

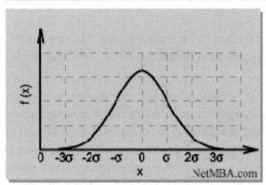

Retrieved from http://www.netmba.com/statistics/distribution/normal/ December, 26, 2010.

Gaussian, Normal, or Bell-Shaped Distribution:

The Gaussian Distribution is arguably the most well known data distribution since large numbers of measures in our physical environment are distributed in this manner such as our height, weight, etc. The data represented by this distribution is composed of either interval or ratio data types which will be discussed later in this text.

Student t Distribution:

Student t Distribution:

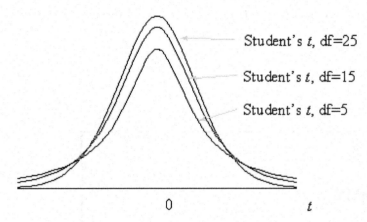

Retrieved from http://www.statsdirect.com/help/distributions/pt.htm December 26, 2010.

The **df** or number of degrees of freedom of this function is calculated by subtracting the number of population parameters that are estimated which is often **one** or the mean of the distribution from the sample size [**df** = n - 1]. When large samples are employed, the distribution approaches the Gaussian, Normal, or Bell-shaped distribution noted above. The data represented by this distribution needs to be either interval or ratio which will be discussed later in this text.

Chi Square Distribution:

Chi Square Distribution:

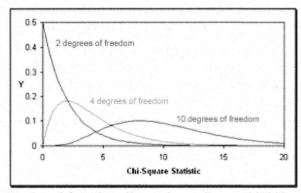

Retrieved from http://stattrek.com/Lesson3/ChiSquare.aspx December 26, 2010.

This distribution will be used later in this text in conjunction with Cross-Tabulations and Chi Square (χ^2) tests. In this instance, the number of degrees of freedom are calculated in the same manner as the Student *t* Distribution which is calculated by subtracting the number of population parameters that are being estimated which is often **one** or the mean of the distribution from the sample size [**df** = n - 1]. The data represented by this distribution can be nominal (categorical) which will be discussed later in this text.

F Distribution:

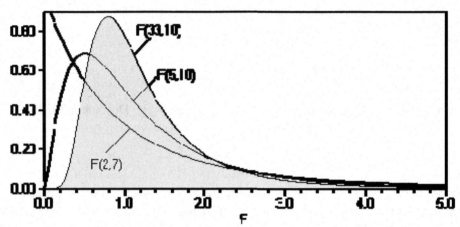

Received from http://www.statistics4u.info/fundstat_eng/cc_distri_fisher_f.html December 26, 2010.

F Distribution:

The final distribution that this text addresses is the F Distribution. Like the other three distributions presented here, this distribution is associated with degrees of freedom. Specifically, this distribution is related to two degrees of freedom which are denoted as df_1 and df_2. Two degrees of freedom are necessary since this technique relates the variance of two separate variables. These degrees of freedom are calculated by subtracting the number of population parameters that are being estimated which is often **one** or in this case two variances of the first distribution from the sample size [$df_1 = n_1 - 1$] and the second distribution from its sample size [$df_2 = n_2 - 1$]. This distribution will be used later in conjunction with the statistical techniques called *Analysis of Variance* and *Regression*. The data represented by this distribution need to be either interval or ratio which will be discussed later in this text.

a. Problems to be Solved with Frequencies

A variety of business and marketing problems can be addressed through an analysis and understanding of data distributions. It is exceptionally important to understand how data is distributed so that researchers use the appropriate statistical techniques to analyze the data they receive. Frequencies of counts are extremely important especially when the only data type available is nominal/categorical. For example, variables such as gender, colors of a particular product, or housing types are instances of variables for which data types other than nominal/categorical cannot be developed. In these instances, the **mode** is the appropriate measure of what is known as central tendency. The mode is the number that is repeated most often in a list or sample of data. This represents the highest column in a histogram or bar chart or the largest segment in a pie chart. Diagrams such as these provide researchers with excellent pictorial representations of data which demonstrate (1) what the mode is or (2) whether more than a single mode exists. Later in this text, it will be demonstrated how an hypothesis might be tested that suggests that one category is significantly larger than another category. The interpretation of the results of36

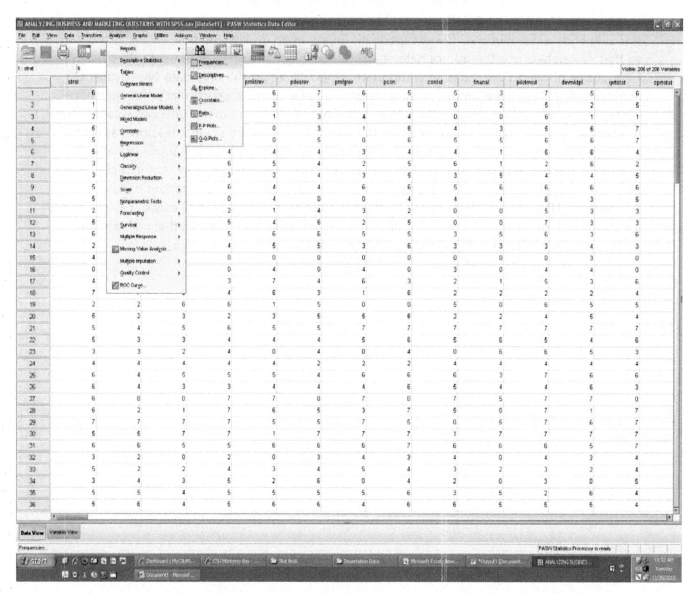

Then click on a variable of interest in the left hand window. In this case ***prodtype*** was selected. ***prodtype*** is a variable name for Product Type. Six product types appeared in this dataset. They include (1) new-to-the-world, (2) new-to-the-firm, (3) line extension, (4) product improvement, (5) cost reduction, and (6) repositioning. This variable represents the counts of the various new product types reported in a research study. Click on the *Statistics* button in the Frequencies window and select *Mode* in the *Frequencies: Statistics* window. Click on *Continue*.

such statistical tests as well as the interpretation of bar charts, histograms, and pie charts depend on the variables involved, and the experience and knowledge of the researcher(s).

b. Frequencies Examples

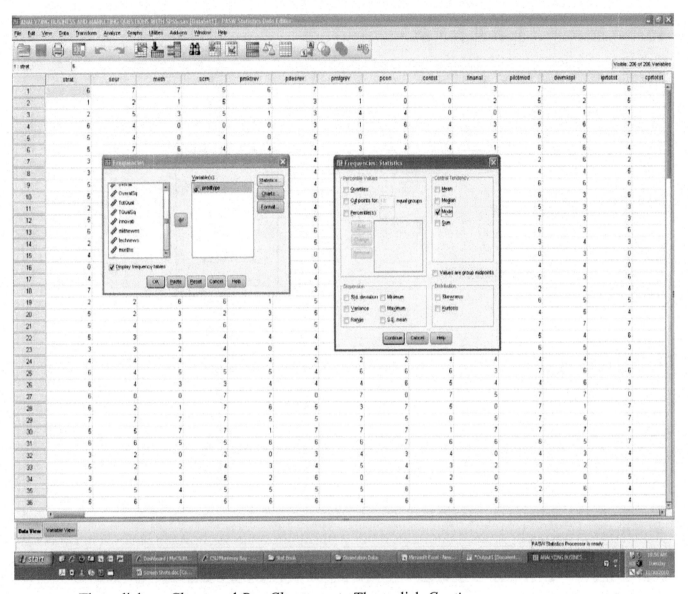

Then click on *Charts* and *Bar Charts* next. Then, click *Continue*.

The following SPSS screen shots, diagrams, and statistical outputs depict the how a researcher can analyze data using frequency counts or percentages of nominal/categorical data. The first set of screen shots depict how one would analyze nominal/categorical data using the SPSS Frequencies function. To arrive at the SPSS screen shot below, click on *Analyze* on the menu bar and then click on *Descriptive Statistics* on the first drop-down menu and *Frequencies* on the second drop-down menu.

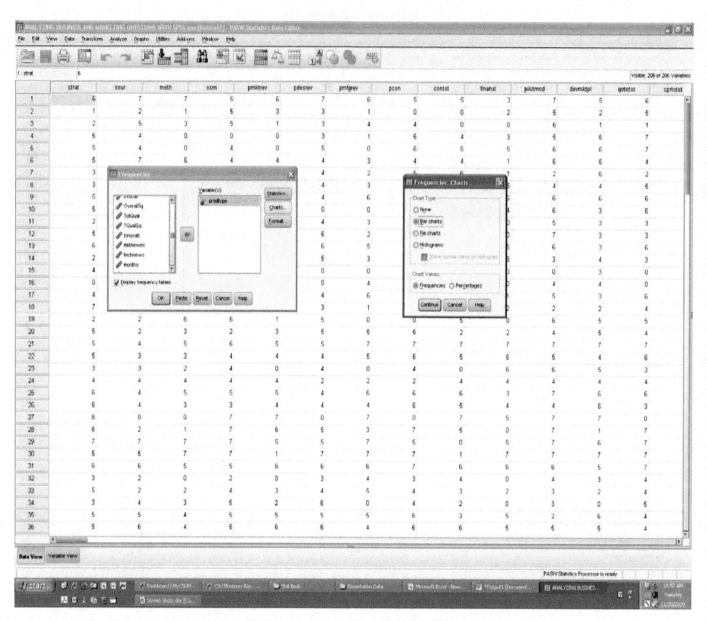

The output of the *Frequencies* process can be found in the next views.

```
GET
  FILE='C:\Documents and Settings\mill6391\Desktop\MyStuff\Research\Dissertati
on Data\MurrayScaledDissDataSPSS-11-29-2010.sav'.
DATASET NAME DataSet1 WINDOW=FRONT.
FREQUENCIES VARIABLES=prodtype
  /STATISTICS=MODE
  /BARCHART FREQ
  /ORDER=ANALYSIS.
```

Frequencies

[DataSet1] C:\Documents and Settings\mill6391\Desktop\MyStuff\Research\Dissert
ation Data\MurrayScaledDissDataSPSS-11-29-2010.sav

Statistics

prodtype

N	Valid	131
	Missing	0
Mode		3

prodtype

		Frequency	Percent	Valid Percent	Cumulative Percent
Valid	1	16	12.2	12.2	12.2
	2	38	29.0	29.0	41.2
	3	41	31.3	31.3	72.5
	4	28	21.4	21.4	93.9
	5	3	2.3	2.3	96.2
	6	5	3.8	3.8	100.0
	Total	131	100.0	100.0	

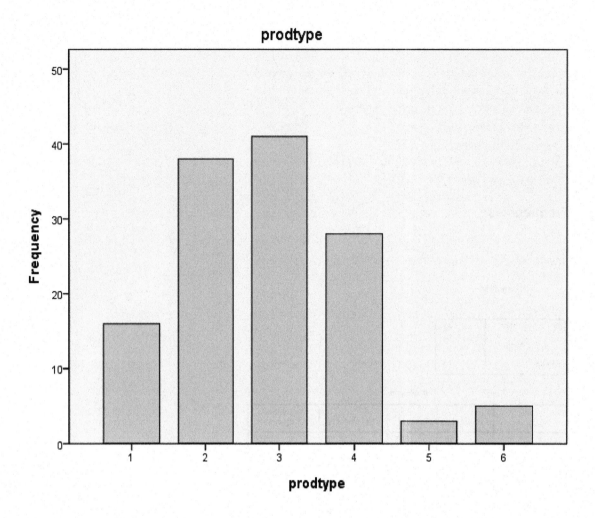

The following Excel screen shots, diagrams, and statistical outputs depict how a researcher can analyze data using frequency counts or nominal/categorical data. The data pertaining to the variable of interest needs to be situated on an Excel spreadsheet as noted in the following spreadsheet along side the column that describes the values that are found in the variable of interest. These values need to be nominal/categorical, ordinal, or interval data types but not ratio/continuous data. In this case, the variable data is depicted by a 7-point Likert scale. The title of the second column is **bin**. In Excel, click on *Data* on the main menu. Then, click on the *Data Analysis* button on the far right-hand side. In the *Data Analysis* window, locate and click on *Histogram* and then click *OK*.

Next, click on the miniature Excel spreadsheet on the right-hand side of the input window that

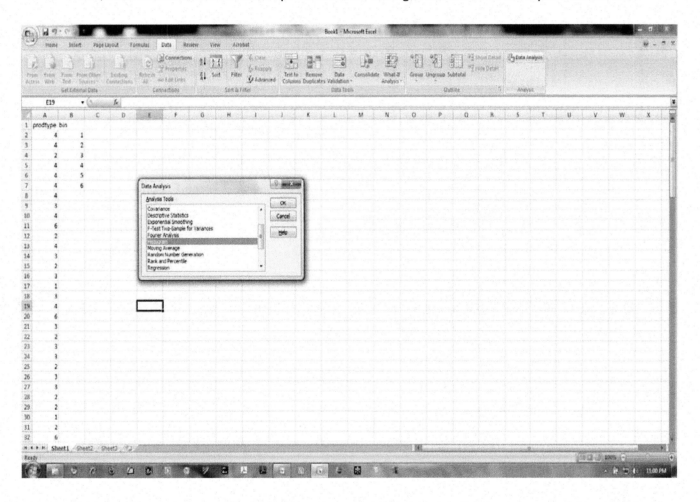

is entitled Input Range. Then, select the data in the column pertaining to the variable of interest including the title as noted in the next screen shot. The Labels box on the *Histogram* dialog box needs to be checked. This allows the *Titles* at the top of the data columns to be selected along with the data in the columns. In this case *prodtype* and *bin*. Click the *Pareto (sorted histogram), Cumulative Percentage, and Chart Output* check boxes.

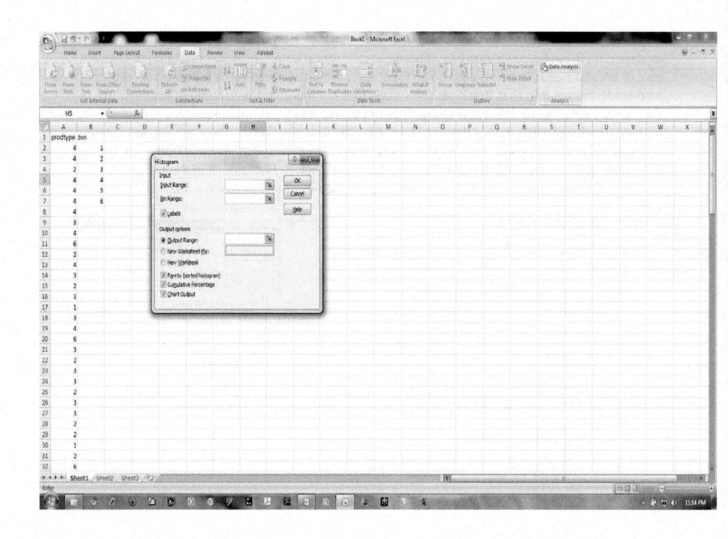

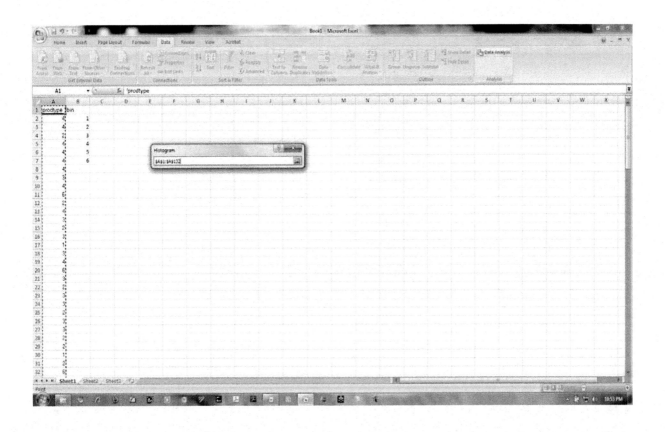

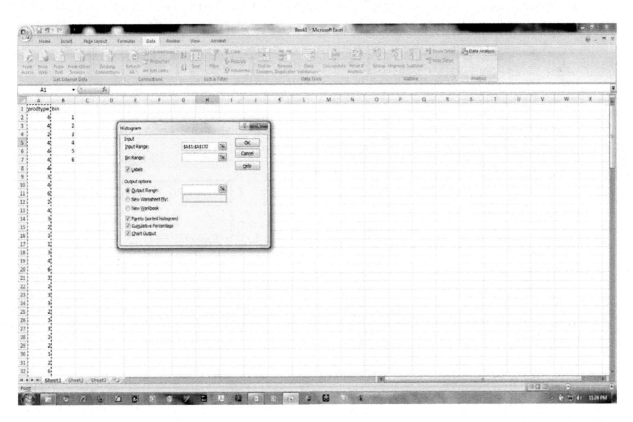

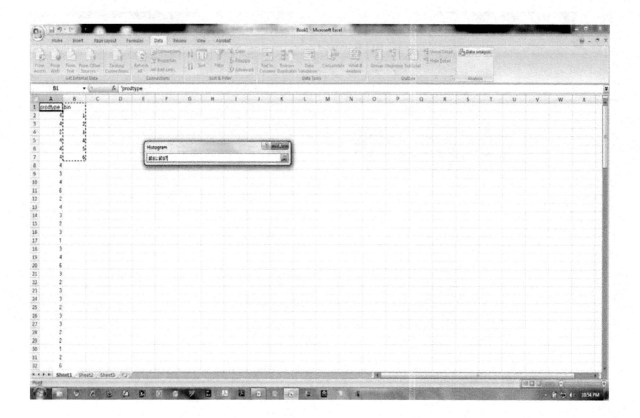

Then, click the Excel spreadsheet icon on the right-hand side of the *Input Range* text box to progress to the reduced *Input Range* text box window to select the **prodtype** data range. Then,

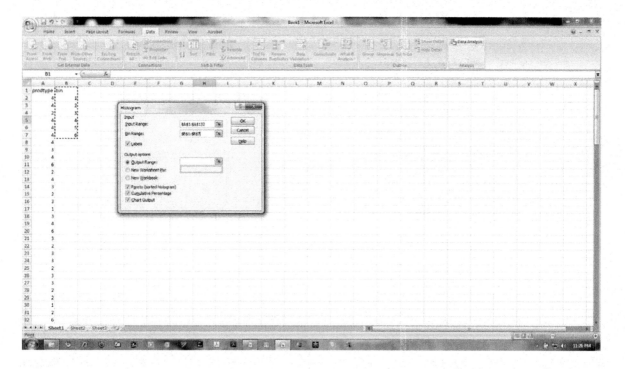

click on the spreadsheet icon on the right-hand side of the *Input Range* text box to progress to the *Histogram* dialog box.

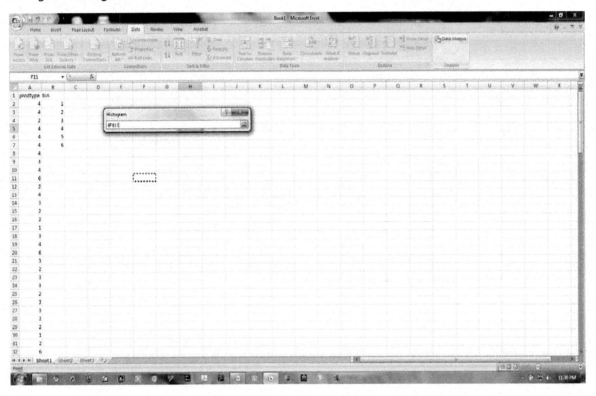

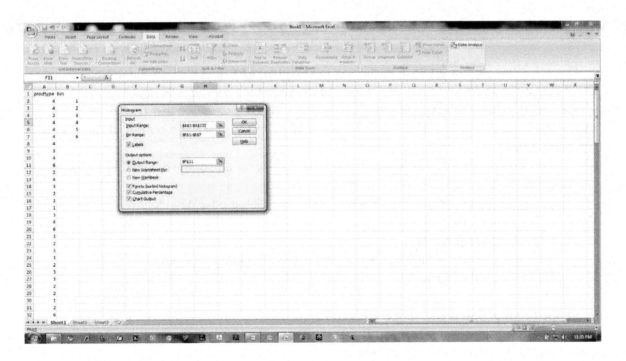

Next, click on the Excel spreadsheet icon next to the *Bin Range* window. Then, select the Bin values.

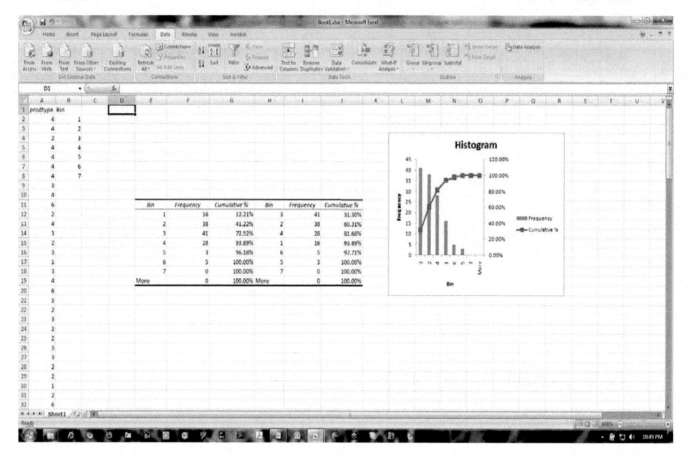

Once the Bin values are selected, click on the Excel Spreadsheet icon on the right-hand side of the reduced histogram window noted below to return to the *Histogram* dialog box.

Next, click on the Excel spreadsheet icon next to the *Output Range* text box. Then, select the upper left-hand corner cell of the area in which you want to place the output of the *Histogram* function values.

Now, click on the Excel Spreadsheet icon on the right-hand side of the reduced *Histogram* dialog box noted below.

Next, the researcher should click *OK* in the *Histogram* dialog box. What follows are the results of the Excel Frequencies/Histogram process.

Findings Using Frequencies:
- No missing values regarding the nominal/categorical variable ***prodtype***
- Mode = 3 (Line extensions)

Implications of Research Using Frequencies:
- Line extensions were the most frequent new product type in the sample with the new-to-the-firm product type not far behind.

G. Descriptive Statistics

a. Problems to be Solved with Descriptive Statistics

Descriptive Statistics provide metrics that depict measures of central tendency, dispersion, and the shape of data distributions. Several *Descriptive Statistics* provide various measures that relate to these three major distribution attributes. Below are SPSS processes that can be used to calculate and present nine such statistics that include mean, range, minimum, maximum, variance, standard deviation, Standard Error of the mean, skewness, and kurtosis.

b. Descriptive Statistics Examples

To arrive at the SPSS screen shot below, click on *Analyze* on the menu bar and then click on *Descriptive Statistics* on the first drop-down menu and *Descriptives* on the second drop-down menu.

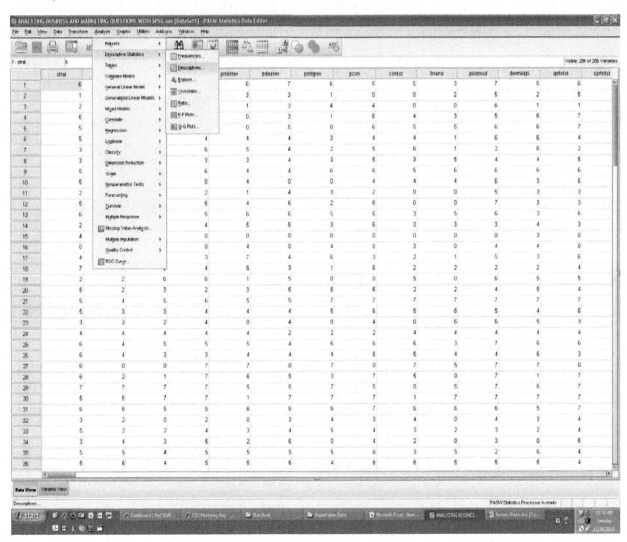

Next, click on the *Options* button and select mean, std deviation, variance, range, minimum, maximum, S E mean (standard error of the mean), skewness, and kurtosis. Then, click *Continue*.

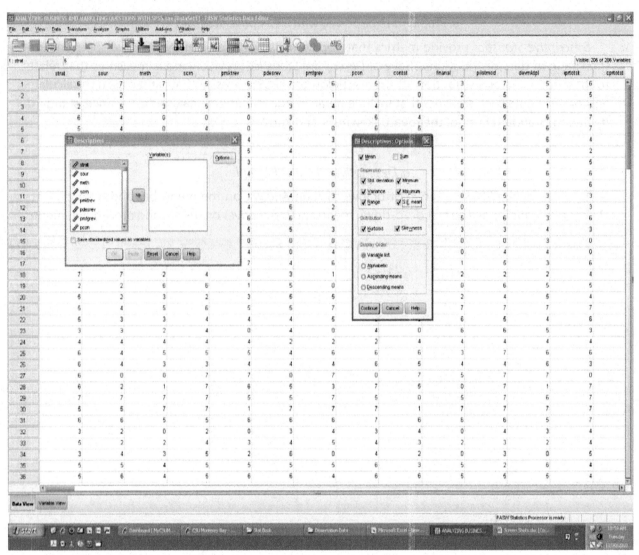

In the window on the left-hand side of the *Descriptives* window select the variables of interest and then click on the arrow between the windows to select and move the selected items to the variables window. In this case the ***pmktrev*** (perceived performance of a preliminary marketing review), ***pdesrev*** (perceived performance of a preliminary design review), and ***pmfgrev*** (perceived performance of a preliminary manufacturing review) are selected.

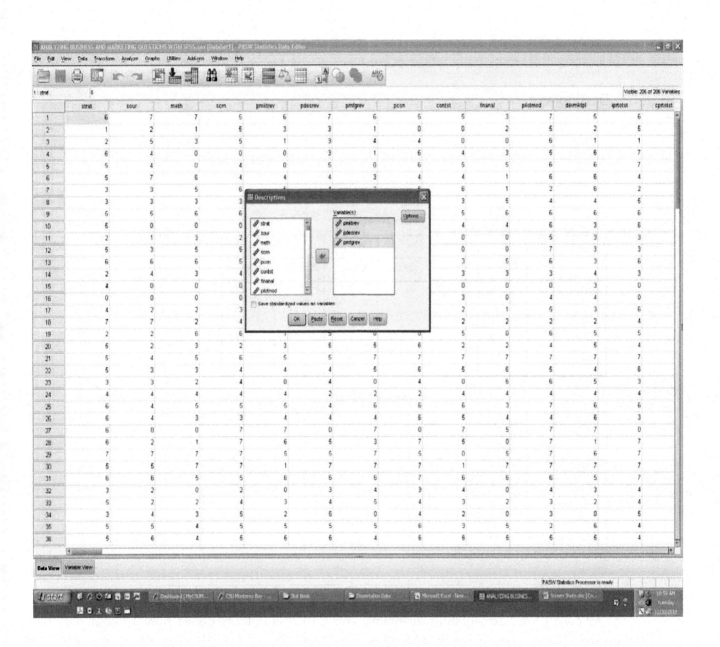

Then click *OK* which produces the following Descriptive Statistics.

```
DESCRIPTIVES VARIABLES=pmktrev pdesrev pmfgrev
  /STATISTICS=MEAN STDDEV VARIANCE RANGE MIN MAX SEMEAN KURTOSIS SKEWNESS.
```

Descriptives

[DataSet1] C:\Documents and Settings\mill6391\Desktop\MyStuff\Research\BOOK MA
TERIALS\New Books\Stat Book\ANALYZING BUSINESS AND MARKETING QUESTIONS WITH SP
SS.sav

Descriptive Statistics

	N	Range	Minimum	Maximum	Mean	
	Statistic	Statistic	Statistic	Statistic	Statistic	Std. Error
pmktrev	131	7	0	7	3.72	.174
pdesrev	131	7	0	7	4.56	.152
pmfgrev	131	7	0	7	3.91	.192
Valid N (listwise)	131					

Descriptive Statistics

	Std. Deviation	Variance	Skewness		Kurtosis	
	Statistic	Statistic	Statistic	Std. Error	Statistic	Std. Error
pmktrev	1.997	3.989	-.520	.212	-.681	.420
pdesrev	1.737	3.017	-.826	.212	.358	.420
pmfgrev	2.199	4.838	-.419	.212	-.979	.420
Valid N (listwise)						

The following Excel screen shots, diagrams, and statistical outputs depict how a researcher can analyze data and create *Descriptive Statistics* using interval or ratio data. The data pertaining to the variables of interest need to be situated on an Excel spreadsheet as noted in the following spreadsheet. In this case, the variable data is depicted by three 7-point Likert scales. The titles of the columns of data to be studied are **pmktrev, pdesrev, and pmfgrev**. These columns of data need to be in adjacent columns in the Excel spreadsheet. In Excel, click on *Data* on the main menu. Then, click on the *Data Analysis* button on the far right-hand side. In the *Data Analysis* window, locate and click on *Descriptive Statistics* and then click *OK*.

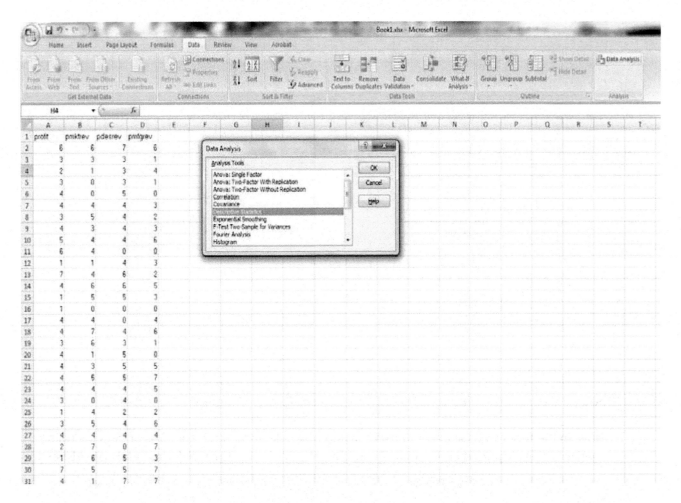

Now, the researcher should select the data in the columns pertaining to the three variables of interest including the titles as noted in the next screen shot. The *Labels* box on the *Descriptives* window needs to be checked. This allows the Titles at the top of the data columns to be selected along with the data in the columns. In this case **pmktrev, pdesrev, and pmfgrev** are those labels. Click the *Summary statistics* and the *Confidence level for Mean* check boxes with 95% entered into the *confidence level for Mean* text box. Next, click on the miniature Excel spreadsheet icon on the right-hand side of the input window that is entitled *Input Range* to move to the reduced *Descriptive Statistics* dialog box.

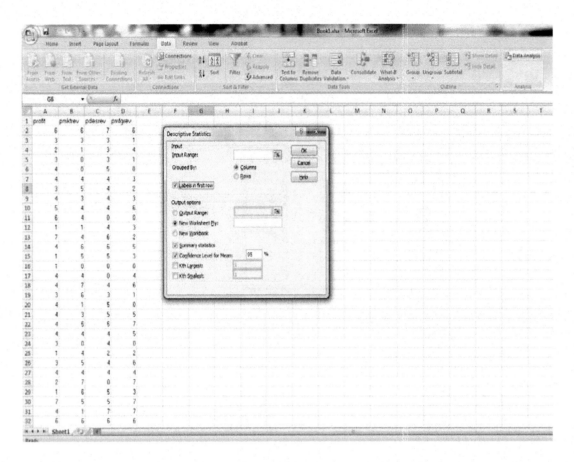

Now, in the reduced *Descriptive Statistics* dialog box, select the three columns of data including the variable titles included in row one. Then, the researcher needs to click the Excel spreadsheet

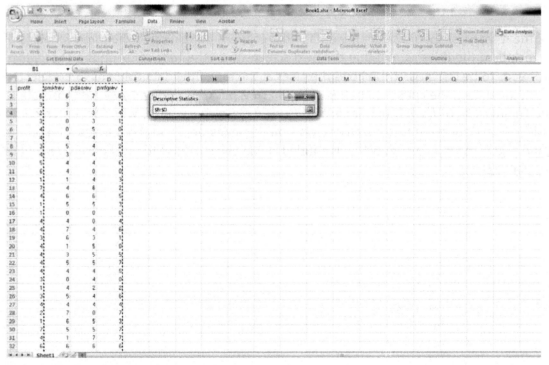

icon on the right-hand side of the *Descriptive Statistics* text box to return to the larger *Descriptive Statistics* dialog box.

In the *Descriptive Statistics* dialog box, click the *Output Range* radio button. Then, click the Excel spreadsheet icon at the right-hand side of the *Output Range* text box to progress to the reduced *Descriptive Statistics* dialog box.

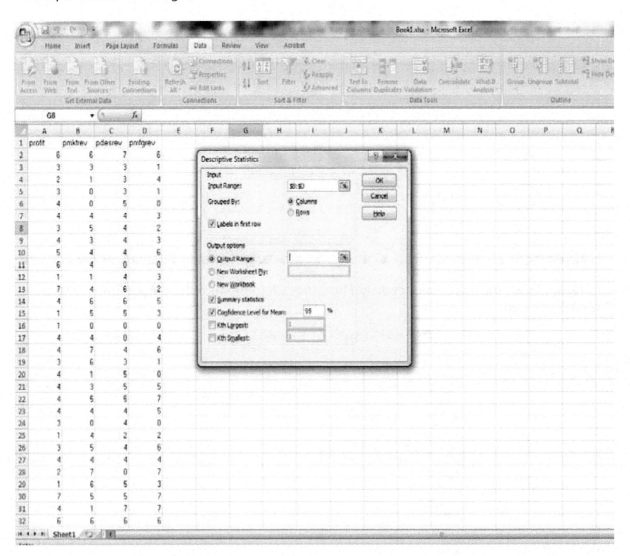

Now, in the reduced *Descriptive Statistics* dialog box, select the upper left-hand corner for the output to be presented on the spreadsheet. Then, the researcher needs to click the Excel spreadsheet icon at the right-hand side of the *Descriptive Statistics* text box. When this is done, click the Excel icon spreadsheet on the right-hand side of the *Descriptive Statistics* text box to return to the primary *Descriptive Statistics* dialog box.

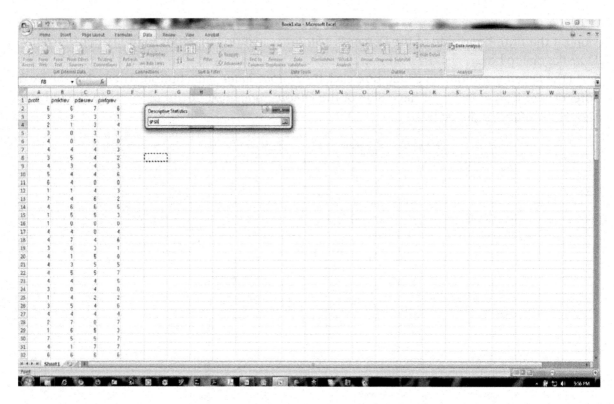

Now, in the *Descriptive Statistics* dialog box, click *OK* to produce the output of the *Descriptive Statistics* process.

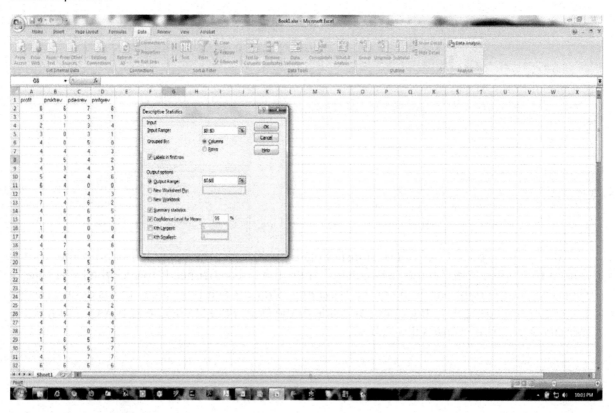

The following presents the results of the Excel *Descriptive Statistics* process.

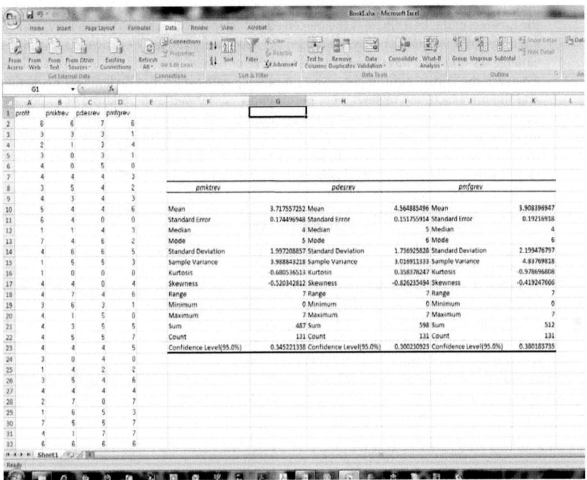

Findings Using Descriptive Statistics:

- **Means** of the three variables
- **Standard errors** of the means for the three variables
- Sample **standard deviation** of the three variables
- Sample **variance** of the three variables
- Sample **Range** of the three variables
- Sample **minimum** of the three variables
- Sample **maximum** of the three variables
- Sample **kurtosis** of the three variables
- Sample **skewness** of the three variables

Implications of Research Using Descriptive Statistics:

- The descriptive statistics presented here describe all the statistics for all of the three variables. The statistics provide information to the researcher regarding the central tendency, the dispersion, and the shape of the distributions for three variables. In these instances, the perceived proficiency with which a preliminary design review was performed was viewed as the greatest or the best whereas the perceived proficiency with which a preliminary marketing review was viewed as being performed the least or the worst. The skewness of all three variable distributions was skewed to the negative or lowest side (long tail of a distribution). However, the kurtosis of the perceived proficiency with which the preliminary marketing and the manufacturing reviews were performed were viewed as leptokurtic or to possess positive kurtosis whereas the perceived proficiency with which the preliminary design review was performed was viewed as platykurtic or to possess negative kurtosis. Additionally, the dispersion of the distribution of the preliminary manufacturing review variable was the largest whereas the preliminary design review variable was the smallest.

H. References

Cook, T.D. and Campbell, D.T. (1979). Quasi-Experimentation: Design and Analysis for Field Settings. Rand McNally, Chicago, Illinois.

Experimental Design Web Site, Retrieved from http://www.okstate.edu/ag/agedcm4h/academic/aged5980a/5980/newpage2.htm January 5, 2011.Formulating Hypotheses

http://apps.who.int/medicinedocs/fr/d/Jwhozip14e/9.html

http://www.netmba.com/statistics/distribution/normal/

http://www.statsdirect.com/help/distributions/pt.htm

http://stattrek.com/Lesson3/ChiSquare.aspx

http://www.statistics4u.info/fundstat_eng/cc_distri_fisher_f.html

Chapter 2

Inferential Statistics: Formulating and Testing Hypotheses

A. Formulating Hypotheses

As previously stated in Chapter 1, theory is often thought to be the depiction in a pictorial or linguistical manner of a particular arrangement of concepts. Theories can be *general statements* developed from evidence, facts, laws, and/or predictions, or they can be *general statements* that have been tested to some degree and are thought to be widely accepted. Hypotheses on the other hand are most often specifically constructed statements that relate concepts in a particular manner. Hypotheses are developed to test portions or entire theories and can be thought of as educated guesses or questions which are structured as statements. The next few paragraphs describe the selection and development of three of several types of hypotheses that can be created.

To create hypotheses, the researcher needs to first develop *Research Questions* and *Research Objectives*. Research Questions guide the research process and their answers lead to achieving the objectives of the research. It is fair to assume that two products for example engender the same degree of loyalty unless you have evidence to support an alternative hypothesis. Assume that $\bar{x}_1$ is the mean loyalty statistic for a product such as a brand of instant coffee determined from a survey of instant coffee drinkers that will be called brand #1 for this example. Also, assume that $\bar{x}_2$ is the mean loyalty statistic for another brand of instant coffee determined from the same survey of instant coffee drinkers that will be called brand #2 for this example. Therefore, what is known as a NULL hypothesis or *strawman statement*, might be $H_0: (\bar{x}_1 - \bar{x}_2) = 0$. This NULL hypothesis suggests that the means of the loyalty measures of the two instant coffee brands derived from this hypothetical data sample are statistically the same. For this example, the alternative or research hypothesis (H_A) would indicate that the means of the two sets of loyalty measurements are unequal. There are two additional hypothesis forms other than the means being equal from which to choose which are (1) $H_0: (\bar{x}_1 - \bar{x}_2) \le 0$ and (2) $H_0: (\bar{x}_1 - \bar{x}_2) \ge 0$. Note that the equal condition ($=$) is always found in the NULL hypothesis whether it is accompanied by a $>$ or $<$ condition or not. In the instance in which the NULL hypothesis is $H_0: (\bar{x}_1 - \bar{x}_2) = 0$, the Alternative or Research hypothesis (H_A) is $H_A: (\bar{x}_1 - \bar{x}_2) \ne 0$. However, when the NULL hypothesis is either (1) $H_0: (\bar{x}_1 - \bar{x}_2) \le 0$ or (2) $H_0: (\bar{x}_1 - \bar{x}_2) \ge 0$, the corresponding Alternative or Research hypothesis is (1) $H_A: (\bar{x}_1 - \bar{x}_2) > 0$ or (2) $H_A: (\bar{x}_1 - \bar{x}_2) < 0$ respectively.

When NULL hypotheses are created that suggest means are equal, the tests that result are called *two-tailed tests.* However, when NULL hypotheses are created that suggest means are greater than or equal to, or less than or equal to each other, the tests that are performed are called *one-tailed tests.*

For example, a researcher might state his or her NULL and Alternative hypotheses regarding the relationship between the means of instant coffee brand loyalty as H_0: $(\bar{x}_1 - \bar{x}_2) \leq 0$ and H_A: $(\bar{x}_1 - \bar{x}_2) > 0$. If $\bar{x}_1$ represents the loyalty mean of Folgers instant coffee and $\bar{x}_2$ represents the loyalty mean of Maxwell House instant coffee, the NULL hypothesis can be stated in words as the loyalty mean of Folgers instant coffee is statistically less than or equal to the loyalty mean of Maxwell House instant coffee whereas the Alternative or Research hypothesis in words in this example is the loyalty mean of Folgers instant coffee is statistically greater than (or preferred to) the loyalty mean of Maxwell House instant coffee.

B. Alpha [α] (Type I Error Significance Value) and *p*-values (Observed Significance Level)

Type I error significance value (α) is a metric that is selected by the researcher. This metric represents the amount of error that a researcher is willing to accept while testing an hypothesis. The α value that is typically employed is 0.05 which represents a 5% probability that the NULL hypothesis under examination will be rejected *when the NULL hypothesis is actually true.* Additionally, an α of 5% can be depicted as the area under a normal/Gaussian/bell-shaped curve which resides in one or both tails under the curve and represents the *rejection region* for testing hypotheses. In other words, if research identifies a difference between two means that results in a probability or *p* value that is less than α or 0.05, the researcher should *reject* the NULL hypothesis. If research identifies a difference between two means that results in a probability or *p* value that is greater than or equal to α or 0.05, the researcher should *fail to reject* the NULL hypothesis. When a researcher rejects a NULL hypothesis, it is often stated that the Alternative or Research hypothesis is supported by the study evidence. As noted above, a one-tailed test places all 5% in a single tail of the normal distribution whereas a two-tailed test places 2.5% in each of the two tails of the normal distribution.

C. Hypothesis Testing Process

To perform effective research, researchers need to follow a process to test to test hypotheses and answer Research Questions that lead to Research Objectives. The following list of activities prescribes a path for researchers to follow to create and test hypotheses.

a. Specify the Population(s) of Interest

At the outset of a research process, a researcher needs to create Research Questions as noted earlier. Research Questions are based on salient issues that stem from problems, opportunities, and/or general gaps in knowledge. Such questions can be reduced to inquires regarding concepts and relationships among concepts that need to be measured and understood to answer the Research Questions. When the appropriate concepts and relationships are identified, suitable populations can be recognized from which to develop samples and gather data. The hypothesis development process needs to be completed prior to the survey development and data gathering processes.

b. Formulate Null and Alternative Hypotheses

Once a researcher understands the Research Questions that need to be addressed, and the concepts and relationships that are relevant to those questions he or she has the information to formulate NULL and Alternative hypotheses. Such hypotheses are formed based on theory and suppositions that researchers have about the concepts and their relationships as they influence the objectives of a particular research study. Developing research hypotheses requires a researcher to recognize the situation that appears to be true unless compelling evidence is found to believe otherwise. Specific NULL and Alternative hypotheses are specifically formed using the processes described above.

c. Specify the Type I Error Significance Level

Using the thought process described above involving Type I errors, a researcher needs to select a Type I error metric with which they are comfortable. This specifically means that a researcher needs to select an Alpha [α] which can be used to test hypotheses. As noted earlier, an Alpha [α] of 0.05 or 5% is typically selected unless there is a compelling reason to employ an Alpha [α] which is either smaller or larger.

d. Construct the Rejection Region and Decision Rule

The hypotheses developed in (b) above and the specification of an acceptable Type I error (Alpha [α]) per the information in (c) above form the basis for the construction of a rejection region(s) and a decision rule(s). The appropriate *rejection region* can be developed from the construction of either two-tailed or one-tailed hypotheses and the specification of a Type I error level. If two-tailed hypotheses are formed, the Type I error and rejection region is equally apportioned to two areas under the normal curve. If one-tailed hypotheses are formed, the Type I error and rejection region is assigned to a single area in either the left or right tail under the normal curve. Therefore, the appropriate decision rule is to reject a NULL hypothesis if the calculated *p* value is in most cases less than Alpha [α] or the calculated test statistic is in most cases greater than the tabled statistic that is associated with the chosen acceptable Type I error level.

e. Calculate the Appropriate Test Statistic

Depending on what is being tested (two means, more than two means, variances, etc.), the researcher needs to calculate a test statistic such a *t*, F, χ^2, or other statistic. Test statistics can be calculated using the appropriate formulae or making use of statistical software packages such as SPSS or Excel. When test statistics are calculated, they need to be reported by the researcher along with the *p* value associated with the calculated test statistics.

f. Reach a Test Decision by Comparing the Calculated Test Statistic with a Tabled Test Statistic or a p Value with a Selected Alpha [α] Value

After the appropriate test statistics are calculated, the researcher needs to compare either the calculated p value with the selected Alpha [α] or compare the calculated test statistic with the appropriate tabled test statistic. When using statistical software packages such as SPSS and Excel, it is often easiest to compare calculated p values with the selected Alphas [α] however in some instances, such as SPSS, p values related to one-tailed t tests are not provided. In these instances, it will be shown later in this volume that a researcher needs to compare calculated test statistics with tabled test statistics to make a test decision.

g. Draw a Conclusion

Hypothesis test conclusions are made based on the results of tests that are the consequence of the gathering and processing of evidence. Therefore, in most cases, if resulting p values are less than the selected Alpha [α] values or calculated test statistics are greater than tabled test statistics, researchers need to *reject* stipulated NULL hypotheses. If resulting p values are greater than or equal to the selected Alpha [α] values or calculated test statistics are less than or equal to tabled test statistics, researchers need to *fail to reject* NULL hypotheses.

D. Comparing Means

The comparison of means is a major mechanism for researchers to perform tests of hypotheses and answer Research Questions. Researchers use several forms of hypotheses to make comparisons of means including the ones described earlier. It is important to remember that to calculate means researchers need to possess either interval or ratio data. The discussion of hypothesis testing that follows, and involves a comparison of means illuminates the use of tests and test statistics including t-tests and F-tests. It will be demonstrated that t-tests are used in a variety of tests that compare two means or a single mean and a fixed parameter. The use of F-tests to compare more than two means will also be discussed and the testing process will be demonstrated.

a. Comparing Two Means-t-Statistics

Hypothesis testing with the use of t-tests allows researchers to understand whether the means of two variables are equivalent or whether the mean of a single variable is equal to a specified population parameter or measure.

1. t-Statistics-One Sample t-test

What immediately follows is the use of t-tests to determine whether the mean of a data distribution is equivalent to a single value that might represent a population parameter or some other fixed value/number. The basic formula to calculate a t-statistic follows.

$t = (\bar{x} - \mu) / (s_{\bar{x}})$ where the denominator $(s_{\bar{x}})$ represents the standard deviation of the sampling distribution of the mean, $\bar{x}$ represents the mean of a distribution of data, and μ represents a population parameter or measure.

Therefore, $s_{\bar{x}} = s/\sqrt{n}$ --- where s = the standard deviation of the sample data and n = sample size.

This particular formula creates a *t*-statistic by comparing the mean of a single variable to a specified population parameter or measure (μ).

2. One Sample *t*-test Examples and Problems to be Solved

Examples of problems, opportunities, and knowledge gaps for which hypothesis testing using single sample *t*-tests are appropriate include:

- Comparing the mean of a distribution of data representing *loyalty to a brand* to a known measure of brand loyalty to determine whether the sample distribution of data appears to have come from the same population as the known mean.
- Comparing the mean of a prior year's *customer satisfaction* mean to the mean of a new sample of satisfaction data.
- Comparing the *purchase intention* for a prior product model with the mean of survey data related to a current year's product model.

The following SPSS screen shots, diagrams, and statistical outputs depict how a researcher can analyze data using one sample *t*-tests. The first set of screen shots depicts how one would analyze scaled (interval or ratio) data using the SPSS *Compare Means* function and *One Sample t Tests*. To arrive at the SPSS screen shot below, click on *Analyze* on the menu bar and then click on *Compare Means* on the first drop-down menu and *One Sample t Test* on the second drop-down menu.

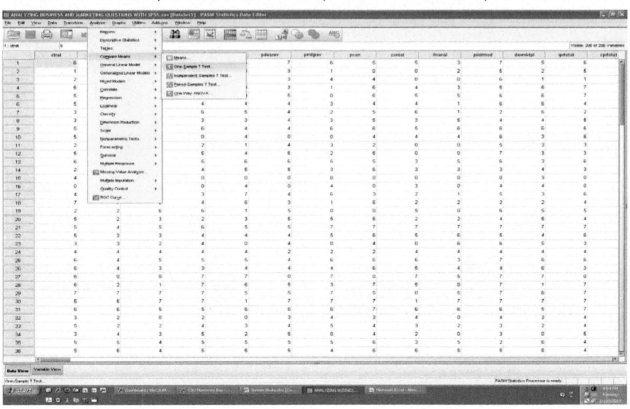

Next, select the data distribution to be investigated from the left window in the *One Sample **t** Test* dialog box. In this case, the **profit** variable is selected. Therefore, the researcher is trying to determine whether a particular sample of firms' profits for particular new product is equivalent to a value of 4 which in this case represents the center point on a 7 point scale. The scale is driven by the statement "This product's profits were *worse/better* than expected" where *worse* is represented by 1 on the scale and *better* is represented by 7. Then, the researcher needs to insert the value 4 in the text window entitled *Test Value*.

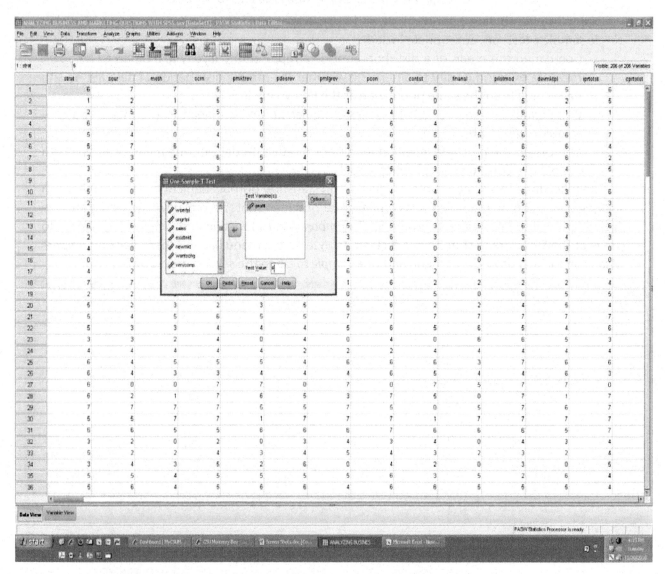

Then, click on *OK*, to produce the SPSS output noted below.

```
T-TEST
  /TESTVAL=4
  /MISSING=ANALYSIS
  /VARIABLES=profit
  /CRITERIA=CI(.95).
```

T-Test

[DataSet1] C:\Documents and Settings\mill6391\Desktop\MyStuff\Research\Dissert
ation Data\MurrayScaledDissDataSPSS-8-9-2010.sav

One-Sample Statistics

	N	Mean	Std. Deviation	Std. Error Mean
profit	131	3.68	1.764	.154

One-Sample Test

	Test Value = 4					
					95% Confidence Interval of the Difference	
	t	df	Sig. (2-tailed)	Mean Difference	Lower	Upper
profit	-2.080	130	.039	-.321	-.63	-.02

Excel does not offer a specific function, as noted in the following, by which the mean of a single data distribution can be compared to a single value that, for example, represents the mean of another data distribution.

Findings Using *One Sample t-tests:*

- $\bar{x}_1$ is the mean of perceived **profit** for a sample of new products; μ is the population mean of perceived **profit** of several new products in the past.

- $H_0: (\bar{x}_1 - \mu) = 0$ or $H_0: (\bar{x}_1 - \mu) \leq 0$ or $H_0: (\bar{x}_1 - \mu) \geq 0$; μ would be a parameter such as the mean of product satisfaction of a population.

- $H_0: (\bar{x}_1 - \mu) = 0$; $H_A: (\bar{x}_1 - \mu) \neq 0$; To assess this hypothesis, the researcher uses the **p** value 0.039 noted in the output and an α of 0.05. In this instance, the null hypothesis would be rejected.

- The calculated **t** value is -2.080. The researcher needs to use a Tabled **t** value for one tailed **t** tests. The researcher needs a Tabled **t** value for n = 131(**df** = 130) and α = 0.05. The Tabled **t** values associated with 100 and 150 degrees of freedom are 1.660 and 1.655 respectively.

- $H_0: (\bar{x}_1 - \mu) \leq 0$; $H_A: (\bar{x}_1 - \mu) > 0$; The information noted above points out that -2.080 is greater than 1.660 or 1.655, therefore the researcher would fail to reject this null hypothesis.

- $H_0: (\bar{x}_1 - \mu) \geq 0$; $H_A: (\bar{x}_1 - \mu) < 0$; The information noted above points out that -2.080 is more negative than -1.660 or -1.655, therefore the researcher would reject this null hypothesis.

Implications of Research Using *One Sample t-tests:*

Depending on which set of hypotheses was being analyzed, the researcher would either reject or fail to reject the appropriate null hypothesis and determine that (1) $\bar{x}_1$ is not statistically equal to μ, (2) that $\bar{x}_1$ is not statistically equal to or greater than m , or (3) that $\bar{x}_1$ is statistically equal to or less than m. Only as determined by the third hypothesis test would the researcher suggest that the current data sample came from the population associated with m.

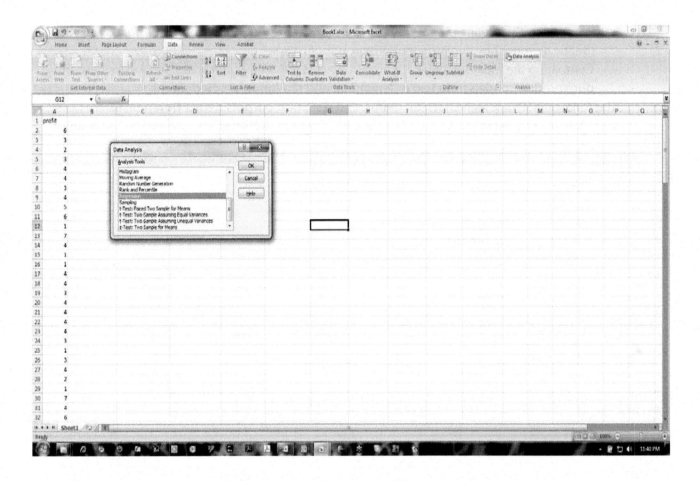

3. *t*-Statistics-Independent Samples *t*-test

The means of two distributions can be compared using *t* statistics and tests as noted earlier. In the first discussion of *t* tests, two items were compared which include the mean of a data distribution and a single number that represents the mean of another distribution. When a researcher is confronted with two distributions of data that are associated with two variables that can be assumed to have no association with one another, the process and function involving Independent Samples *t*-tests of hypotheses should be employed. Therefore, in this instance a researcher is also comparing two items however they comprise the two means of data distributions associated with two statistically independent variables.

4. Independent Samples *t*-test Examples and Problems to be Solved

Examples of problems, opportunities, and knowledge gaps for which hypothesis testing using Independent Samples *t*-tests are appropriate include:
- Comparing the means of data distributions obtained from independent sources representing *loyalty to two brands* of a product category.

- Comparing the means of two data distributions representing *customer satisfaction* for the identical product by two independent groups of people.
- Comparing the means of two data distributions representing *purchase intention* for new and prior product models from two independent and randomly selected samples.

The following SPSS screen shots, diagrams, and statistical outputs depict how a researcher can analyze data using independent *t* tests. The first set of screen shots depicts how one would analyze

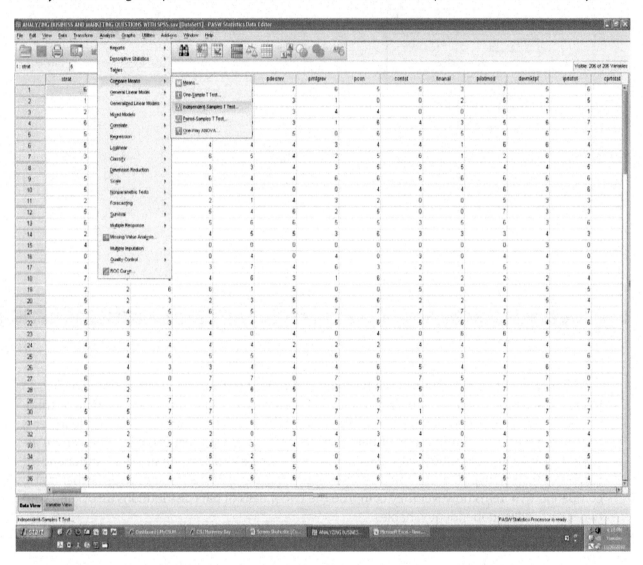

scaled (interval or ratio) data using the SPSS *Compare Means* function and independent *t* tests. To arrive at the SPSS screen shot below, click on *Analyze* on the menu bar and then click on *Compare Means* on the first drop-down menu and *Independent Samples t Test* on the second drop-down menu.

In the *Independent Samples t Test* dialog box move the profit variable from the window on the left to the Test Variables window on the right. Then, move the **morl** variable name to the *Grouping Variable(s)* window and click on the *Define Groups* button. In the *Grouping Variable(s)* dialog box insert the values for the two groups which are represented by the **morl** grouping variable and are specifically 7 and 8 in this instance. The variable **morl** is nominal/categorical data. This variable represents the categories in which the most successful (value =8) and least successful (value=7) products are placed. Therefore, this variable describes the levels of success of the units of analysis in a new product development study. Now click *OK* in the *Define Groups* dialog box and *OK* in the *Independent Samples t Test* dialog box.

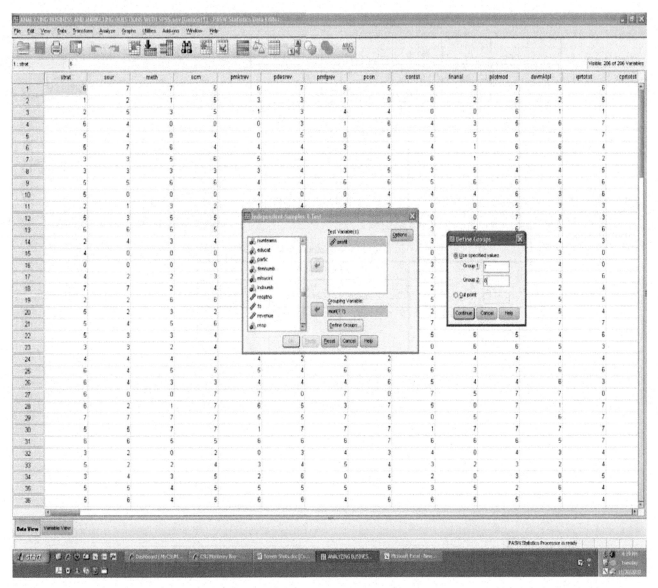

Please note the following to review the SPSS output for an *Independent Samples t Test*.

```
T-TEST GROUPS=morl(7 8)
  /MISSING=ANALYSIS
  /VARIABLES=profit
  /CRITERIA=CI(.95).
```

T-Test

```
[DataSet1] C:\Documents and Settings\mil16391\Desktop\MyStuff\Research\Dissert
ation Data\MurrayScaledDissDataSPSS-8-9-2010.sav
```

Group Statistics

	morl	N	Mean	Std. Deviation	Std. Error Mean
profit	7	59	2.51	1.478	.192
	8	72	4.64	1.356	.160

Independent Samples Test

		Levene's Test for Equality of Variances		t-test for Equality of Means	
		F	Sig.	t	df
profit	Equal variances assumed	1.103	.296	-8.589	129
	Equal variances not assumed			-8.516	119.260

Independent Samples Test

		t-test for Equality of Means		
		Sig. (2-tailed)	Mean Difference	Std. Error Difference
profit	Equal variances assumed	.000	-2.130	.248
	Equal variances not assumed	.000	-2.130	.250

Independent Samples Test

		t-test for Equality of Means	
		95% Confidence Interval of the Difference	
		Lower	Upper
profit	Equal variances assumed	-2.621	-1.640
	Equal variances not assumed	-2.626	-1.635

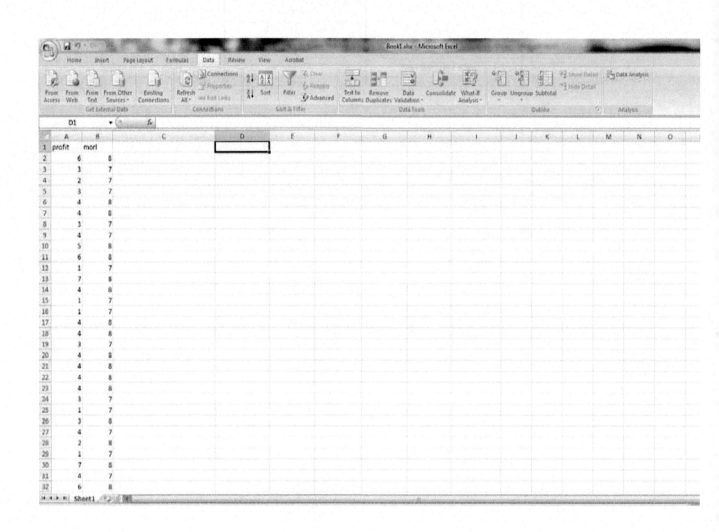

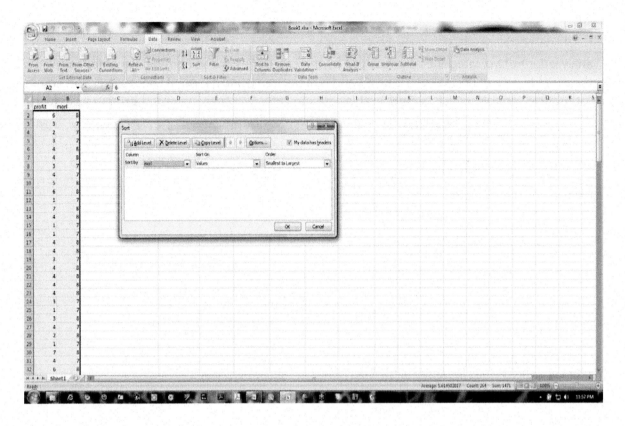

The following Excel screen shots, diagrams, and statistical outputs depict how a researcher can analyze data using *t Tests for Independent Samples*. The data pertaining to the variables of interest needs to be situated on an Excel spreadsheet as noted in the following. One of these variables needs to be scaled (interval or ratio) data. This variable represents the scaled variable to be analyzed. The second variable represents a nominal/categorical data type variable that divides the variables to be

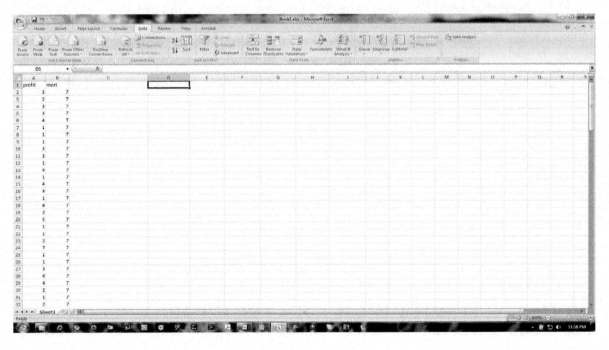

analyzed into two categories represented by the categories of the nominal variable. In this case, the variable data to be analyzed is ***profit*** and is measured using a 7-point Likert scale. The nominal/categorical variable, which is ***morl***, in this case indicates whether the noted ***profit*** was associated

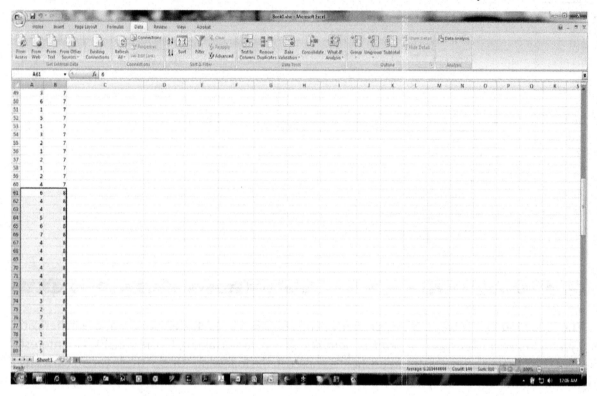

with products that were considered to be either more or less successful by survey respondents.

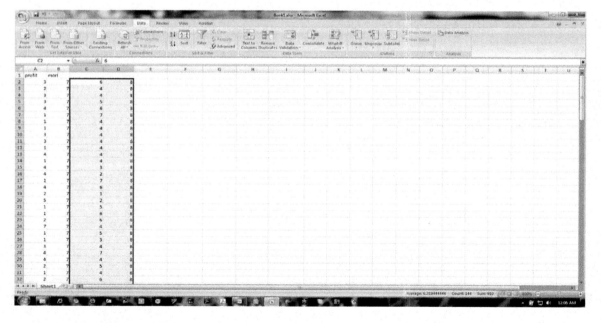

To perform this *t* test in Excel, the researcher needs to place the data in the spreadsheet in the appropriate configuration. The next, screen shot depicts how the data might be found when it is

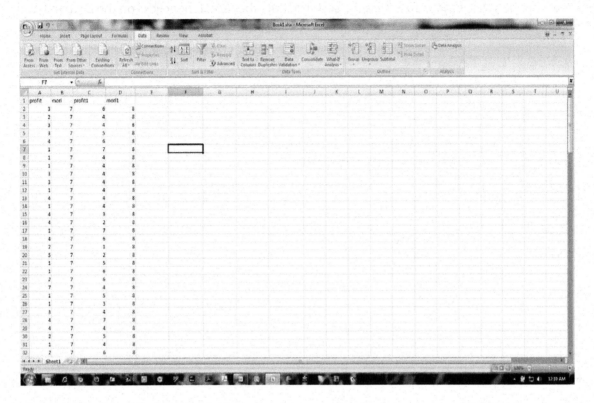

input from survey instruments either in paper or electronic form.

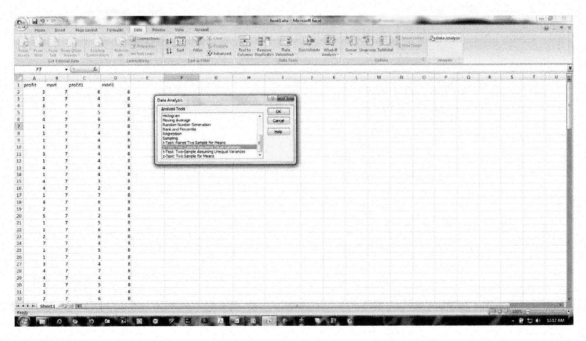

In Excel, to group the survey responses that are associated with scores of 7, which represent less successful products, and scores of 8, which represent more successful products, the researcher needs to use the *sort function*. To access the sort function, the researcher clicks on the *Data* tab and in this case then selects both columns which need to be sorted together. Next, the researcher clicks

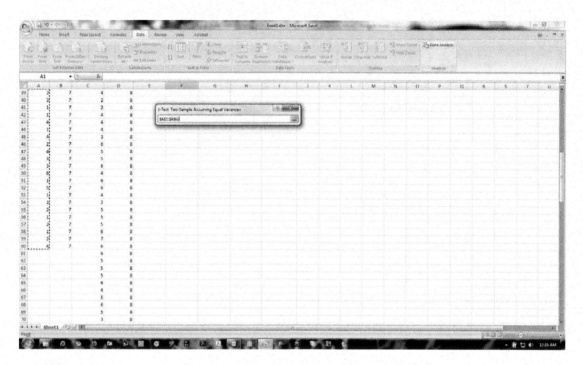

on the *Sort* button to arrive at the configuration noted in the next screen shot.

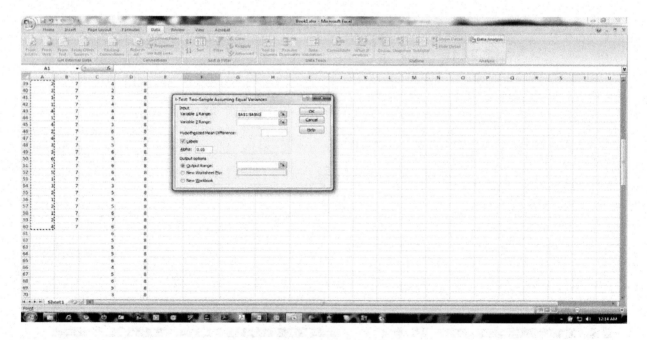

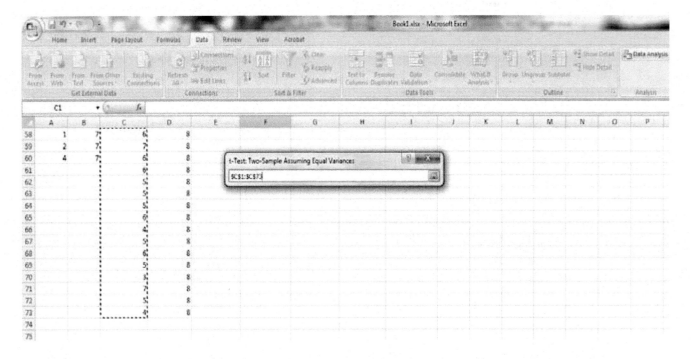

In the *Sort* dialog box, the researcher in this case selects the **morl** variable in the **sort by** drop down menu and then clicks *OK* to arrive at the following screen shot configuration. Now, all of the data points associated with least successful products, which are related to a **morl** value of 7, are listed in the profit column prior to the more successful products which are associated with a **morl** value of 8.

To perform an *Independent Samples **t** test*, the researcher needs to create two more columns on the spreadsheet to align the least successful products with the more successful products.

To do this, the researcher moves the **profit** and **morl** data associated from columns A and B to columns C and D as depicted in the following screen shot.

Now that the data is set up, in Excel, click on *Data* on the main menu. Then, click on the *Data Analysis* button on the far right-hand side of the *Data* menu.

In the *Data Analysis* window, locate and click on **t** *Test: Two Sample Assuming Equal Variances*, as noted below, and then click *OK*.

Now click on the Excel spreadsheet icon on the right-hand side of the *Variable 1 Range* box and select the data in column A to arrive at the following. Click on the Excel spreadsheet icon on the right-hand side of the *Variable 1 Data Range* to return to **t** *Test: Two Sample assuming Equal Variances* dialog box.

Then, click on the Excel spreadsheet icon on the right-hand side of the *Variable 2 Range* box.

Now select the data in column A to arrive at the following.

Click on the Excel spreadsheet icon on the right-hand side of the *Variable 2 Data Range* to return to **t** *Test: Two Sample assuming Equal Variances* dialog box. Be sure that the *Labels* check box is checked if there were variables titles/names in row 1 of each column and you selected row 1 earlier.

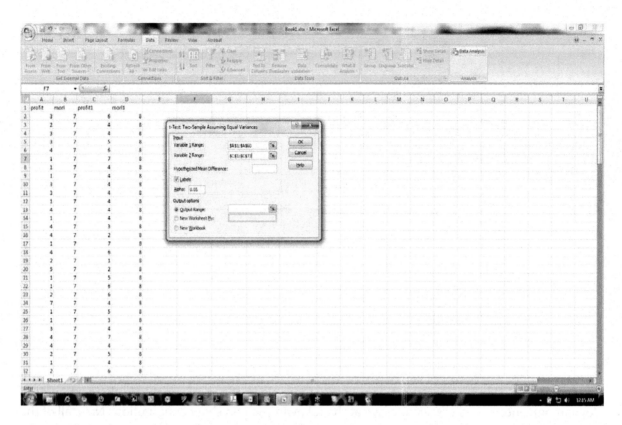

Also, in the next screen shot note that the Alpha needs to be set to 0.05 or whatever value the researcher determines to be appropriate and that the *Output Range* radio button is selected.

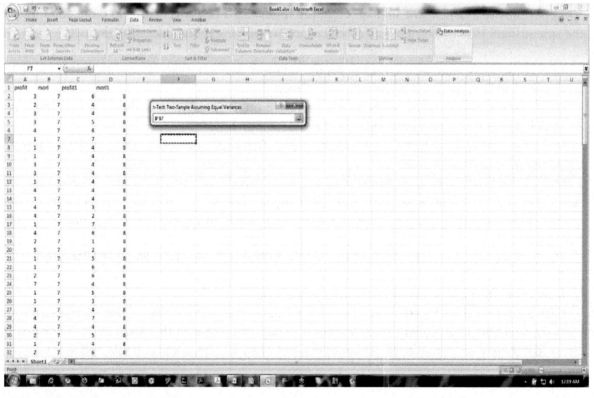

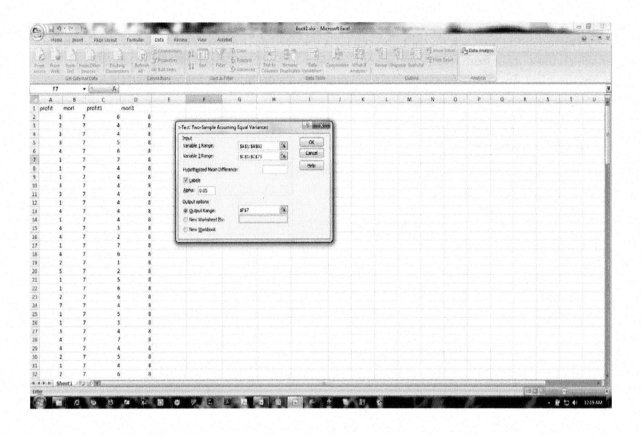

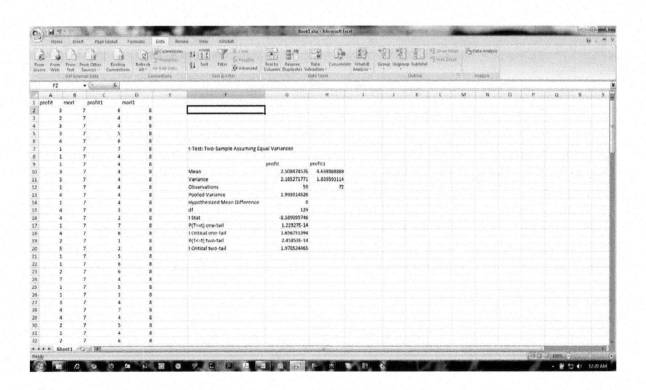

As noted in the next screen shot, the cell F7 is selected as the upper left-hand corner of the area in which the output from this *Independent Samples t Test* will be placed on this spreadsheet.

In the *t Test: Two Sample Assuming Equal Variances* dialog box that follows, click *OK*.

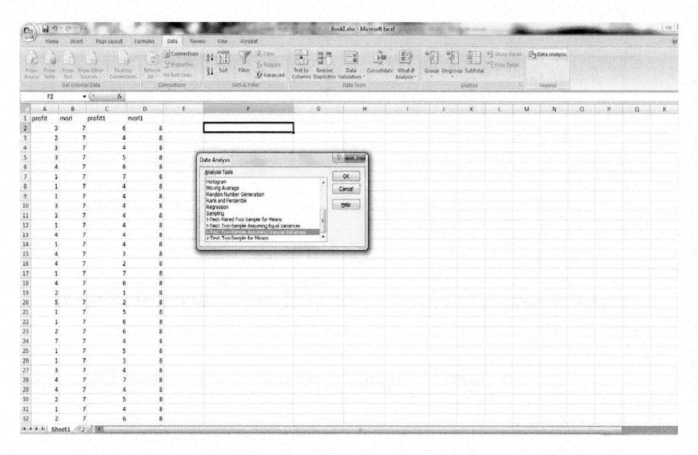

The output from this test can be seen in the next screen shot.

If the researcher obtained or assumed unequal variances regarding the two data sets in question, the researcher would use a *t* Test that is called in Excel a *t Test Two Sample Assuming Unequal Variances*. Therefore, in the *Data Analysis* window, locate and click on *t Test: Two Sample Assuming Unequal Variances*, as noted below, and then click *OK*.

Next, as was presented earlier in the discussion of *t Test: Two Sample Assuming Equal Variances*, click on the Excel icon on the right-hand side of the Variable 1 Range dialog box to get to the reduced *t Test: Two Sample Assuming Unequal Variances* dialog box so that the range can be selected. Also, check the *Labels* check box in the *t Test: Two Sample Assuming Unequal Variances* dialog box.

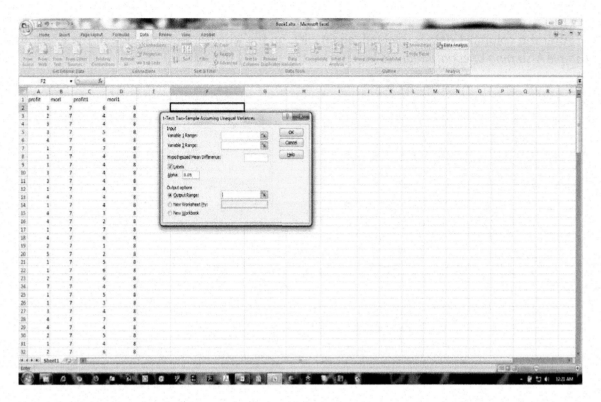

Select the data range in column A along with the title or name in row 1. Click on the Excel icon on the right-hand side of the Variable 1 Range dialog box to return to the primary *t Test: Two Sample Assuming Unequal Variances* dialog box.

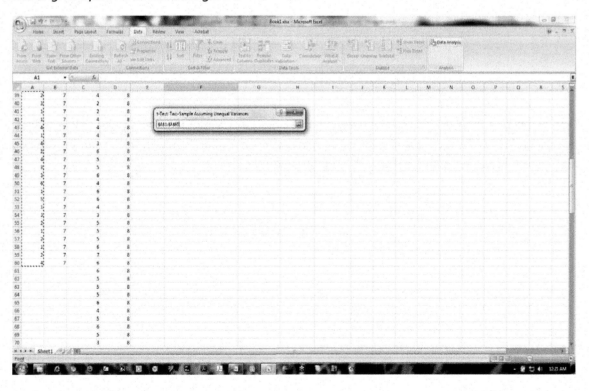

After the column 1 data is selected, again click on the icon on the right side of the **t** *Test: Two Sample Assuming Unequal Variances* to return to the primary dialog box.

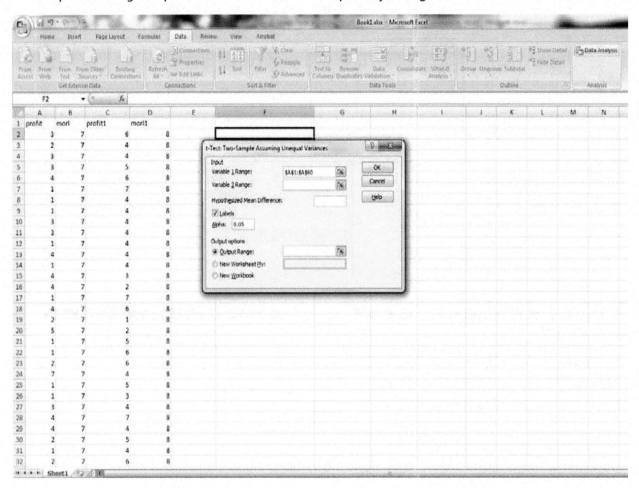

Next, click on the Excel icon on the right-hand side of the Variable 2 Range dialog box to get to the reduced **t** *Test: Two Sample Assuming Unequal Variances* dialog box so that the range 2 data can be selected. Then, select the data for the second variable.

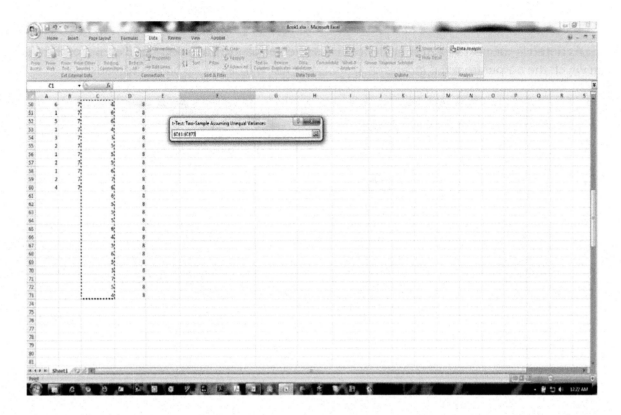

Then click on the Excel icon on the right-hand side of the Variable 2 Range dialog box to get to return to the primary *t Test: Two Sample Assuming Unequal Variances* dialog box. Also, in the next screen shot, assure that Alpha is set to 0.05 or whatever value the researcher determines to be appropriate and that the *Output Range* radio button is selected. Now, click the Excel icon to the right-hand side of the *Output Range* text box.

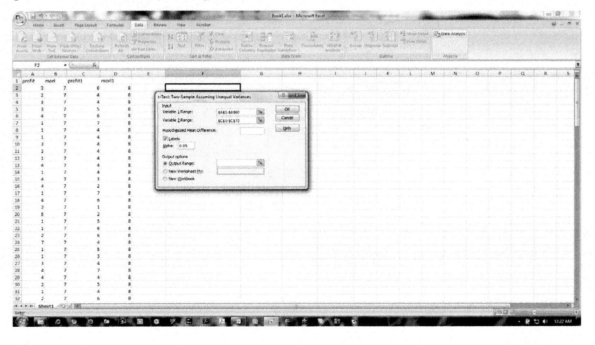

As noted in the next screen shot, the cell F8 is selected as the upper left-hand corner of the area in which the output from this *Independent Samples **t** Test* will be placed on this spreadsheet.

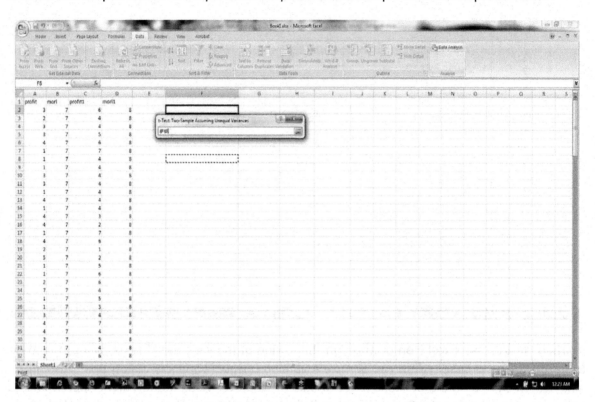

Click *OK* in the following ***t** Test: Two Sample Assuming Unequal Variances* dialog box.

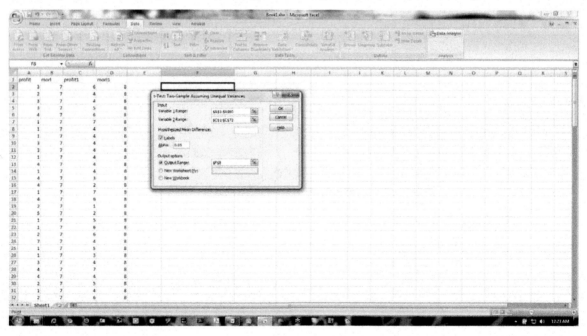

The output from this test can be seen in the next screen shot.

t-Test: Two-Sample Assuming Unequal Variances

	profit	profit1
Mean	2.508474576	4.638888889
Variance	2.185271771	1.839593114
Observations	59	72
Hypothesized Mean Difference	0	
df	119	
t Stat	-8.515636511	
P(T<=t) one-tail	2.99963E-14	
t Critical one-tail	1.657759285	
P(T<=t) two-tail	5.91927E-14	
t Critical two-tail	1.980099853	

- *Findings Using Independent t-tests:*

- $\bar{x}_1$ is the mean profit for new products considered least successful in a sample of new products; $\bar{x}_2$ is the mean profit for new products considered most successful in a sample of new products.

- When employing an Independent t-test in SPSS, the researcher needs to first determine whether the variances are equal. This is done through the analysis of the supplied *F* test statistic and its associated *p* value. Continuing to use an α of 0.05, the researcher would notice that the *F* value is 1.103 and its associated *p* value in this example is 0.296. Therefore, the researcher should fail to reject the null hypothesis (H_0: $\rho_1 = \rho_2$) that the variances of the two data distributions are equal and note that the data supports the equal variance condition.

- H_0: $(\bar{x}_1 - \bar{x}_2) = 0$ or H_0: $(\bar{x}_1 - \bar{x}_2) \le 0$ or H_0: $(\bar{x}_1 - \bar{x}_2) \ge 0$; $\bar{x}_1$ and $\bar{x}_2$ would represent the sample means of two variable distributions such as the mean of product satisfaction for product #1 and the mean of product satisfaction for product #2.

- $H_0: (\bar{x}_1 - \bar{x}_2) = 0$; $H_0: (\bar{x}_1 - \bar{x}_2) \neq 0$; To assess this hypothesis, the researcher uses the **p** value of 0.000 noted in the output and an α of 0.05. In this instance, the null hypothesis would be rejected.

- The calculated **t** value is -8.589 for equal variances and -8515 for unequal variances. The researcher needs to use a Tabled **t** value for one tailed **t** tests. The researcher needs a Tabled **t** value for n = 131(**df** = 129) and $\alpha = 0.05$. The Tabled **t** values associated with 100 and 150 degrees of freedom are 1.660 and 1.655 respectively.

- $H_0: (\bar{x}_1 - \bar{x}_2) \leq 0$; $H_0: (\bar{x}_1 - \bar{x}_2) > 0$; The information noted above points out that -8.589 and -8515 are not greater than 1.660 or 1.655, therefore the researcher would fail to reject this null hypothesis.

- $H_0: (\bar{x}_1 - \bar{x}_2) \geq 0$; $H_0: (\bar{x}_1 - \bar{x}_2) < 0$; The information noted above points out that -8.589 and -8515 are more negative than -1.660 or -1.655, therefore the researcher would reject this null hypothesis.

Implications of Research Using Independent t-tests:

Depending on which set of hypotheses were being analyzed, the researcher would either reject or fail to reject the appropriate null hypothesis and determine that (1) $\bar{x}_1$ is not statistically equal to $\bar{x}_2$, (2) that $\bar{x}_1$ is not statistically equal to or greater than $\bar{x}_2$, or (3) that $\bar{x}_1$ is statistically equal to or less than $\bar{x}_2$. Only as determined by the third hypothesis test would the researcher suggest that the current data samples support the alternative hypothesis. These data suggest (1) that the mean of **profit** for the least successful products in the tested sample is not statistically equal to the mean of **profit** for the most successful products in the tested sample or that (2) that the mean of **profit** for the least successful products in the tested sample is not statistically equal to or greater than the mean of **profit** for the most successful products in the tested sample, however (3) it is suggested that the mean of **profit** for the least successful products in the tested sample is statistically equal to or less than the mean of **profit** for the most successful products in the tested sample.

5. *t*-Statistics-Paired Samples *t*-test

The means of two distributions can be compared using *t* statistics and tests as noted in prior discussions. In the first discussion of *t* tests, two items were compared which include the mean of a data distribution and a single number that represents the mean of another distribution. In the second instance *t* test comparison, two items were compared which were thought to be statistically independent of one another. When a researcher is confronted with two distributions of data that are associated with two variables that can be assumed to associated with one another, the process involving Paired Samples *t*-tests of hypotheses can be employed. Therefore, in this situation a researcher is also comparing two means however they comprise the two means of data distributions that are related to one another in some manner.

6. *Paired Samples t-test Examples and Problems to be Solved*

Examples of problems, opportunities, and knowledge gaps for which hypothesis testing using paired *t*-tests are appropriate include:

- Comparing the means of data distributions obtained from a single respondent from a survey process in which data for two variables have been provided by each of the survey respondents. For example, comparing the *intention to purchase* two different products by respondents of a particular survey process.
- Comparing the means of two data distributions representing *customer satisfaction* related to two restaurants based on data for two satisfaction measurements that have been provided by two distinct survey respondents.
- Comparing the means of two data distributions representing *loyalty* related to two airlines based on data for two loyalty measurements which have been provided by each survey respondent.

The following SPSS screen shots, diagrams, and statistical outputs depict how a researcher can analyze data using paired *t*-tests. The first set of screen shots depict how one would analyze scaled (interval or ratio) data using the SPSS *Compare Means* function and paired *t*-tests. To arrive at the SPSS screen shot below, click on *Analyze* on the menu bar and then click on *Compare Means* on the first drop-down menu and *Paired Samples t Test* on the second drop-down menu.

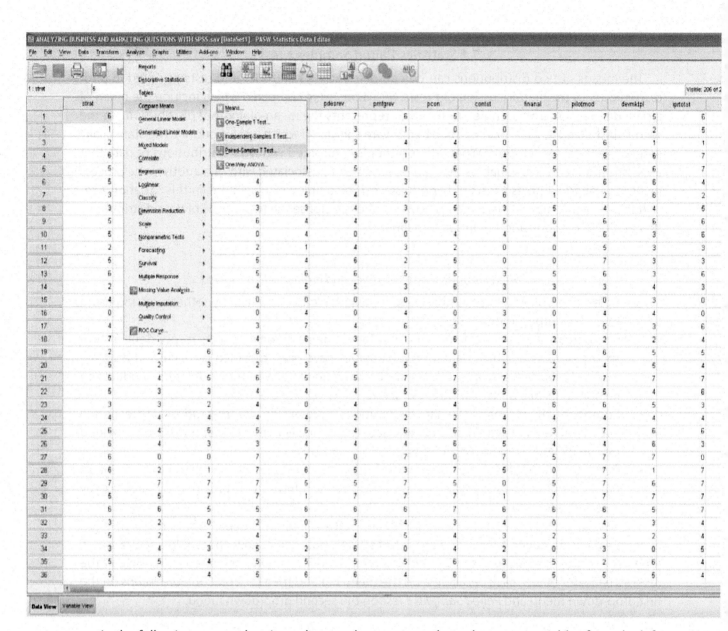

In the following screen shot, it can be seen how a researcher selects two variables from the left-hand window in the *Paired Samples t Test* dialog box and moves them to the right-hand window.

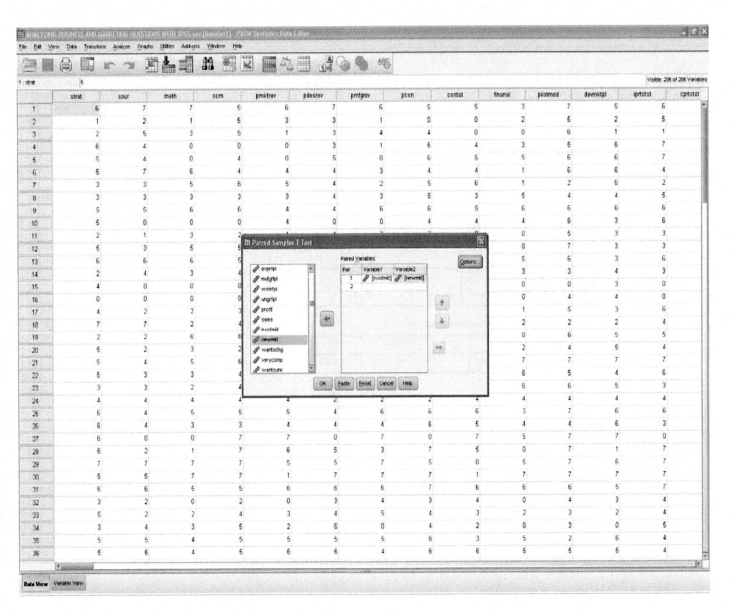

The researcher now clicks *OK* to produce the output found in the following.

```
T-TEST PAIRS=existmkt WITH newmkt (PAIRED)
  /CRITERIA=CI(.9500)
  /MISSING=ANALYSIS.
```

T-Test

[DataSet1] C:\Documents and Settings\mill6391\Desktop\MyStuff\Research\Dissert ation Data\MurrayScaledDissDataSPSS-8-9-2010.sav

Paired Samples Statistics

		Mean	N	Std. Deviation	Std. Error Mean
Pair 1	existmkt	4.53	131	2.160	.189
	newmkt	4.07	131	2.261	.198

Paired Samples Correlations

		N	Correlation	Sig.
Pair 1	existmkt & newmkt	131	.538	.000

Paired Samples Test

		Paired Differences				
					95% Confidence Interval of the Difference	
		Mean	Std. Deviation	Std. Error Mean	Lower	Upper
Pair 1	existmkt - newmkt	.458	2.128	.186	.090	.826

Paired Samples Test

		t	df	Sig. (2-tailed)
Pair 1	existmkt - newmkt	2.464	130	.015

The following Excel screen shots, diagrams, and statistical outputs depict how a researcher can analyze data using *Paired Samples **t** Tests*. The data pertaining to the variables of interest need to be situated on an Excel spreadsheet as noted in the following. To perform a *Paired Samples **t** Test* in Excel does not require the use of a grouping variable as does an *Independent Samples **t** Test*. Both variables portrayed in the following Excel spreadsheet represent the scaled variables to be analyzed. The two variables employed in this example are ***existmkt*** (success entering existing markets with new products) and ***newmkt*** (success opening new markets with new products). Therefore, the researcher is trying to determine whether a particular sample of firms are more successful opening new markets with new products or entering existing markets with new products.

To perform this ***t*** test in Excel, the researcher needs to place the data in the spreadsheet in the appropriate configuration. The next screen shot depicts the variables of interest situated next to one another. Then, in the *Data Analysis* window, locate and click on ***t** Test: Paired Two Sample for Means*, as noted below, and then click *OK*.

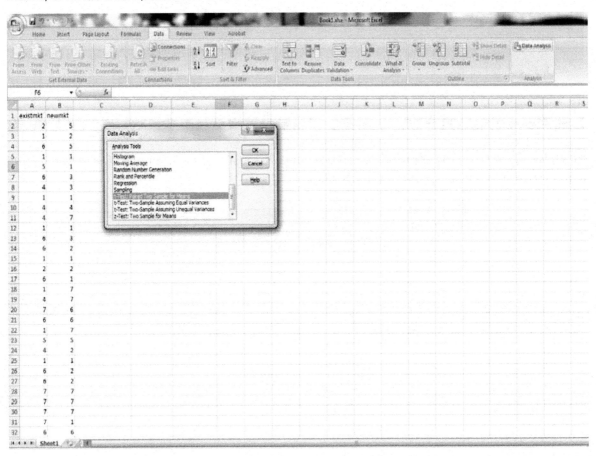

Now the researcher needs to click on the Excel spreadsheet icon on the right-hand side of the *Variable 1 Range* box to reveal the reduced ***t** Test: Paired Two Samples for Means dialog box*. The researcher needs to be sure that the *Labels* check box is checked if row 1 of each column contains the name of the variable(s) being investigated. The researcher should also make sure that the value

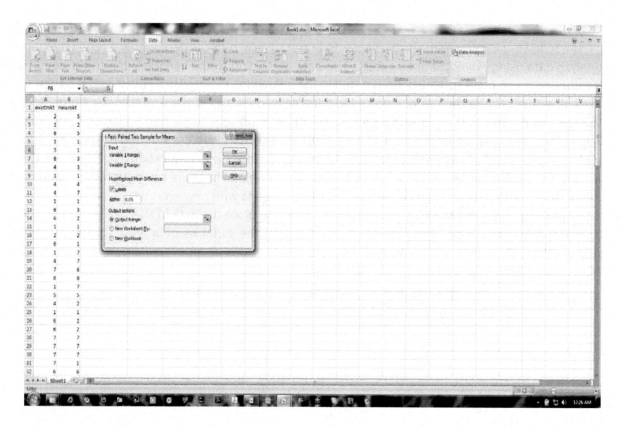

for Alpha is inserted in the appropriate test box which in most cases is 0.05 unless the researcher has a good reason to select a different value for Alpha.

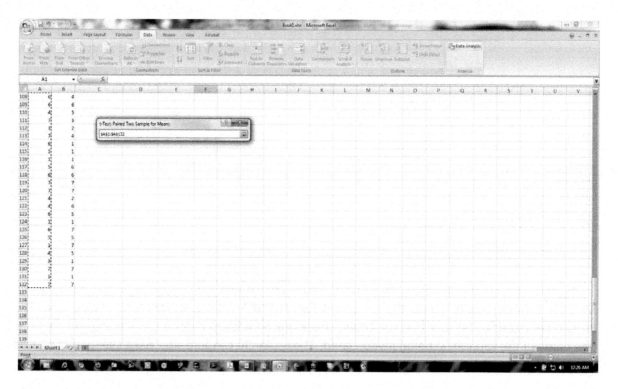

The researcher now needs to select the data in column A to arrive at the following. After selecting the data for the first variable, the researcher needs to click on the Excel spreadsheet icon on the

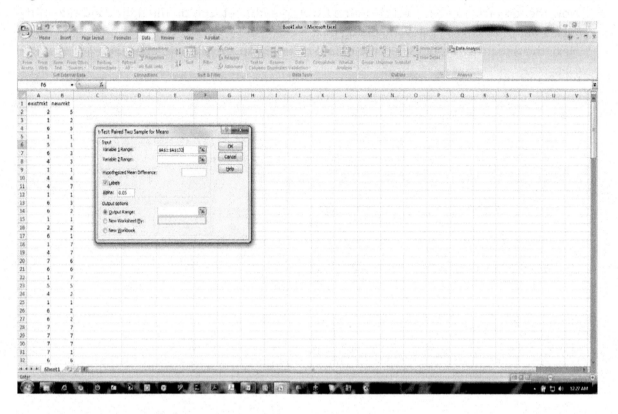

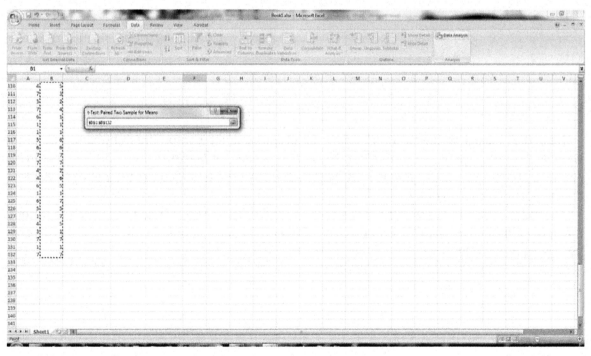

right-hand side of the *Variable 1 Data Range* to return to *t Test: Paired Two Sample for Means* dialog box.

Now the researcher needs to click on the Excel spreadsheet icon on the right-hand side of the *Variable 2 Range* box in the following dialog box.

Next, the researcher should select the data in column B to arrive at the following.

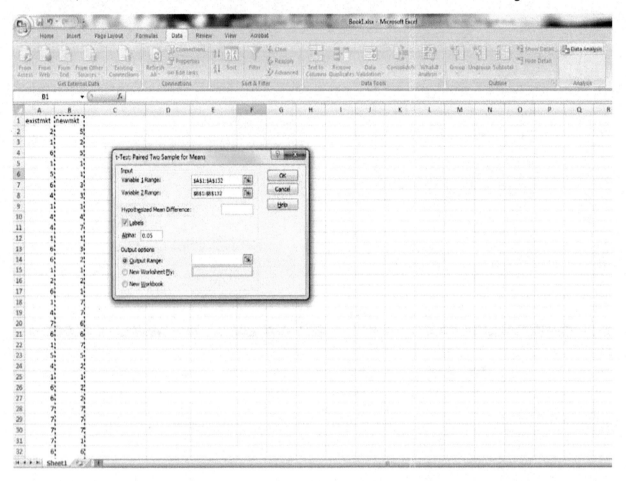

Now, the researcher needs to click on the Excel spreadsheet icon on the right-hand side of the *Variable 2 Data Range* to return to *t Test: Paired Two Sample for Means* dialog box. The researcher needs to click on the *Output Range* radio button and then the Excel icon at the right-hand side of the *Output Range* dialog box.

The following indicates that the researcher needs to click in the selected cell which represents the upper left-hand corner of the output area of the *t Test Paired Sample for Means* test. In this case, the selected cell is D8.

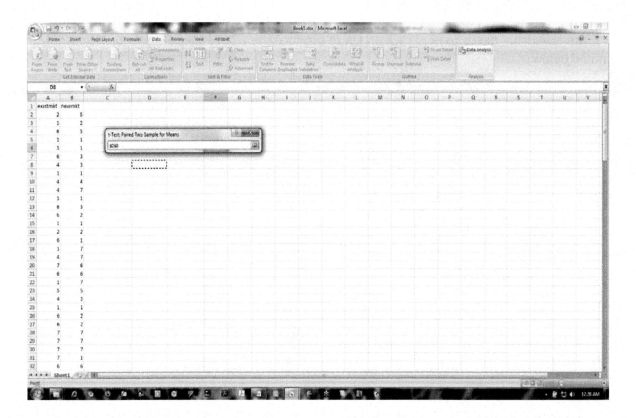

The researcher should now click on the Excel icon of the right-hand side of the *t Test Paired Sample for Means* dialog box to return to the primary *t Test Paired Sample for Means* dialog box.

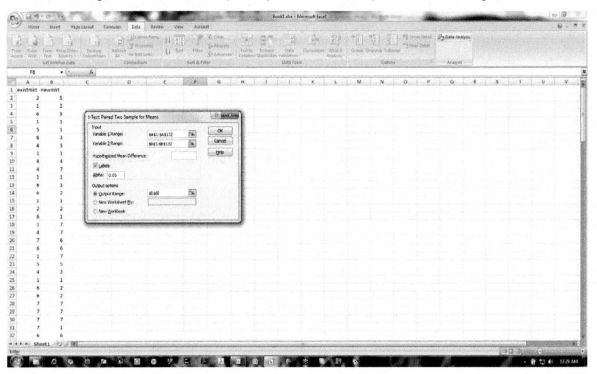

The researcher needs to now click on OK to produce the **t** *Test Paired Sample for Means* output noted below.

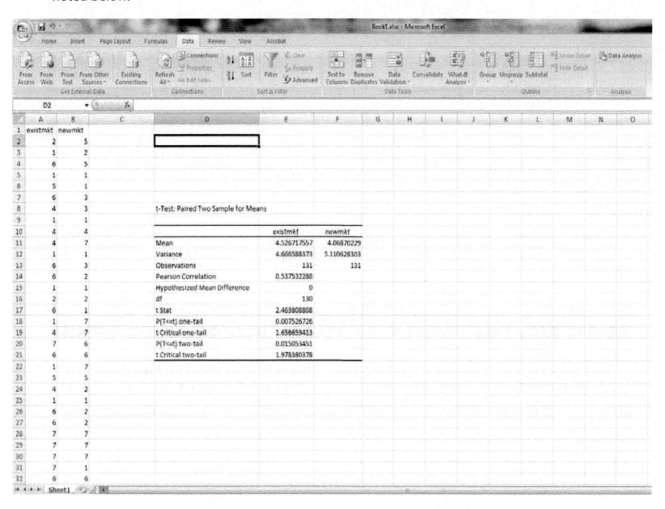

*Findings Using Paired **t**-tests:*

- $\bar{x}_1$ = mean success of a new product entering an existing market; $\bar{x}_2$ = mean of the success of a new product opening a new market.

- $H_0: (\bar{x}_1 - \bar{x}_2) = 0$ or $H_0: (\bar{x}_1 - \bar{x}_2) \leq 0$ or $H_0: (\bar{x}_1 - \bar{x}_2) \geq 0$; $\bar{x}_1$ and $\bar{x}_2$ would represent the sample means of two variable distributions such as the mean of the success of a new product entering an existing market compared to the mean of a new product opening a new market.

- $H_0: (\bar{x}_1 - \bar{x}_2) = 0$; $H_A: (\bar{x}_1 - \bar{x}_2) \neq 0$; To assess this hypothesis, the researcher uses the **p** value of 0.015 noted in the output and an α of 0.05. In this instance, the null hypothesis would be rejected.

- The calculated **t** value is 2.484. The researcher needs to use a Tabled **t** value for one tailed **t** tests. The researcher needs a Tabled **t** value for n = 131(**df** = 130) and α = 0.05. The Tabled **t** values associated with 100 and 150 degrees of freedom are 1.660 and 1.655 respectively.

- $H_0: (\bar{x}_1 - \bar{x}_2) \leq 0$; $H_A: (\bar{x}_1 - \bar{x}_2) > 0$; The information noted above points out that 2.484 is greater than 1.660 or 1.655, therefore the researcher would reject this null hypothesis.

- $H_0: (\bar{x}_1 - \bar{x}_2) \geq 0$; $H_A: (\bar{x}_1 - \bar{x}_2) < 0$; The information noted above points out that 2.484 is not more negative than -1.660 or -1.655, therefore the researcher would fail to reject this null hypothesis.

Implications of Research Using Paired t-tests:

Depending on which set of hypotheses was being analyzed, the researcher would either reject or fail to reject the appropriate null hypothesis and determine that (1) $\bar{x}_1$ is not statistically equal to $\bar{x}$ (2) that $\bar{x}_1$ is statistically equal to or greater than $\bar{x}_2$, or (3) that $\bar{x}_1$ is not statistically equal to or less than $\bar{x}_2$. Only, as determined by the second hypothesis test, would the researcher suggest that the current data samples support the alternative hypothesis. This data suggests (1) that the mean of ***success of a new product entering an existing market*** is not statistically equal to the mean of the ***success of a new product opening a new market*** in the tested sample or that (2) that the mean of ***success of a new product entering an existing market*** is statistically equal to or greater than the mean of the ***success of a new product opening a new market*** in the tested sample, however (3) it is suggested that the that the mean of ***success of a new product entering an existing market*** is not statistically equal to or less than the mean of the ***success of a new product opening a new market*** in the tested sample.

b. Comparing More Than Two Means

1. Analysis of Variance (ANOVA)

Analysis of Variance (ANOVA) is a process by which researchers can compare more than two means. To perform an ANOVA analysis, a researcher needs to study a variable that is, or can be, divided into three or more categories based on the various categories of a nominal variable. This process examines the variability of the data within each category of the nominal variable to perform the test. Specifically, ANOVA compares the variability between the various groups to determine whether all of the means of the groups are equal.

The null hypothesis related to an ANOVA test suggests that ALL of the means of the categories of the nominal variable of interest are equal. This produces the following hypothesis.

H_0: $\mu_1 = \mu_2 = \mu_3 = \ldots = \mu_k$ where k is the number of categories of the nominal variable under study.

H_A: At least one of the means is not statistically equal to the other means.

ANOVA uses an **F** statistic and its associated p value in addition to its associated distribution to make the comparisons among the various categories of the variable under study. The **F** test only suggests whether the means are all equal or not. It does not provide any information regarding which means are different and which means are the same. To shed some light on potential differences in means, the researcher needs to perform *post hoc* tests. A *post hoc* test is only necessary if the null hypothesis is rejected and the *F* test suggests that all means are not equal. There are several post hoc tests that have been suggested by statisticians. The particular *post hoc* test that will be used here is known as the Duncan test.

2. ANOVA examples and problems to be solved

- ANOVA can be used to compare the means of measures of *satisfaction* for the services provided by a tax preparation firm for clients of the tax preparation firm who are divided into categories by their educational level determined by their completion of various years and/or degrees of schooling.
- ANOVA can also be used to compare the means of measures of *intention to purchase* a new model of automobile by potential purchasers of new automobiles who are divided into categories by their income level measured by their stated monthly disposable income.
- In addition ANOVA can be used to investigate whether *brand loyalty* is equivalent across people who reside in various areas of a city or a region. *Brand loyalty* is the metric that is assessed across people in the various geographical areas to be studied.

The following SPSS screen shots, diagrams, and statistical outputs depict how a researcher can analyze data using ANOVA. The first set of screen shots depict how one would analyze scaled (interval or ratio) data using the SPSS *Compare Means* function and *One Way ANOVA Tests*. To arrive at the

SPSS screen shot below, click on *Analyze* on the menu bar and then click on *Compare Means* on the first drop-down menu and *One Way ANOVA Tests* on the second drop-down menu.

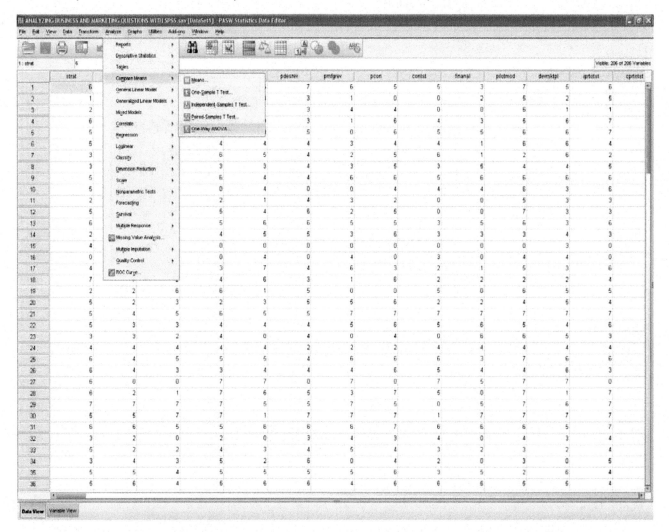

To perform an SPSS *One Way Analysis of Variance*, a researcher needs to select the primary scaled variable of interest. That variable is moved from the left-hand window in the One Way ANOVA dialog box to the right-hand window in the dialog box. In case, the selected variable is ***profit***. The profit measurement is driven by the statement "This product's profits were *worse/better* than expected" where *worse* is represented by 1 on the scale and *better* is represented by 7. Next, the researcher should move the categorical variable to the *Factor* text box. Click on the *Post Hoc* button. When the *One Way Post Hoc Multiple Comparison* dialog box opens, click on the Duncan check box and assure that the Significance Level is set to 0.05 or whatever Alpha level the researcher desires. Then, click *Continue* in the *One Way Post Hoc Multiple Comparison* dialog box and then click OK in the *One Way ANOVA* dialog box.

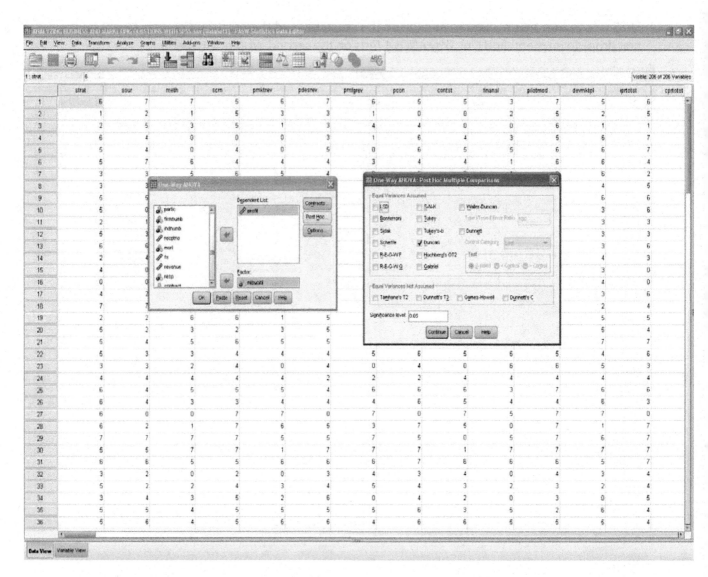

The following is the output of a *One Way ANOVA* procedure in addition to a *Duncan Post Hoc* test. This ANOVA test has resulted in an *F* statistic of 14.779 with an associated *p* value of 0.000. This *p* value is less than 0.05 which means that the researcher should reject the null hypothesis that all of the six group means are equal. Therefore, the researcher should continue to the *Duncan Post Hoc* test to determine which groups have larger and smaller means. The *Duncan Post Hoc* test indicates that groups 1, 3, and 5 should be considered to have equivalent means with a *p* value of 0.253. Groups 4 and 6 are considered to have equivalent means with a *p* value of 0.709. And, groups 2 and 6 are considered to have equivalent means with a *p* value of 0.083. It should be recognized that means can be present in multiple groups however not all of the means in a group can be present in another group or the two groups would collapse into a single group.

```
ONEWAY profit BY mlsucinI
  /MISSING ANALYSIS
  /POSTHOC=DUNCAN ALPHA(0.05).
```

Oneway

```
[DataSet1] C:\Documents and Settings\mill6391\Desktop\MyStuff\Research\Dissert
ation Data\MurrayScaledDissDataSPSS-8-9-2010.sav
```

ANOVA

profit

	Sum of Squares	df	Mean Square	F	Sig.
Between Groups	150.297	5	30.059	14.779	.000
Within Groups	254.238	125	2.034		
Total	404.534	130			

Post Hoc Tests

Homogeneous Subsets

profit

Duncan[a,b]

mlsucinI	N	Subset for alpha = 0.05		
		1	2	3
1	15	2.27		
3	25	2.56		
5	20	2.80		
4	33		4.33	
6	20		4.50	4.50
2	18			5.28
Sig.		.263	.709	.083

Means for groups in homogeneous subsets are displayed.

a. Uses Harmonic Mean Sample Size = 20.511.

b. The group sizes are unequal. The harmonic mean of the group sizes is used. Type I error levels are not guaranteed.

The following Excel screen shots, diagrams, and statistical outputs depict how a researcher can analyze data using *Analysis of Variance (ANOVA) Tests*. The data pertaining to the variables of interest need to be situated on an Excel spreadsheet as noted in the following. To perform what Excel calls an *ANOVA Single Factor* test in Excel requires the use of two variables. The two variables that are portrayed in the following Excel spreadsheet comprise a scaled variable and a nominal/categorical variable. The two variables employed in this example are **profit** (The profit scale is based on the statement "This product's profits were *worse/better* than expected" where *worse* is represented by 1 on the scale and *better* is represented by 7.) and **mlsucinl** (a nominal/categorical variable that encompasses six groups which represent the most and least successful new products developed by three different industries). Therefore, the researcher is trying to determine whether there are differences among the perceived profits of new products relative to what has been observed as the most and least successful new product in the three industries. The researcher needs to click on the Data menu to access the *Sort* icon and the *Data Analysis* icon as noted below.

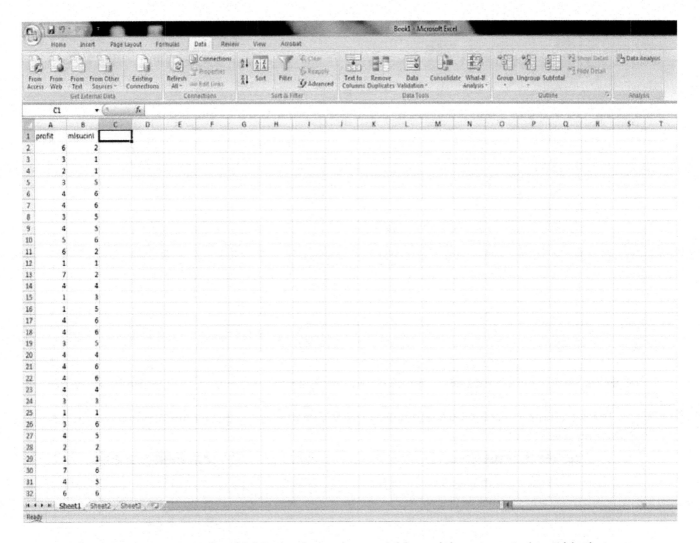

The data represent **profit**, which is the dependent variable, and the categorical variable that represents the three industries and the two groups within each industry to which the profits pertain. These data comprise six groups of **profit** figures that are associated with the three industries and the most and least successful products produced by the firms in these industries captured by this sample. These two columns of data need to be reformatted to perform the ANOVA analysis in Excel. The two columns of data need to be **sorted based on the categorical variable**. To sort this data, the researcher selects the two columns of data and then clicks on the *Sort* icon on the *Data* menu. When the two columns are sorted, separate the columns of data, which in this case represent the perceived **profits** earned by the individual products thought of as either least or most successful in those three industries.

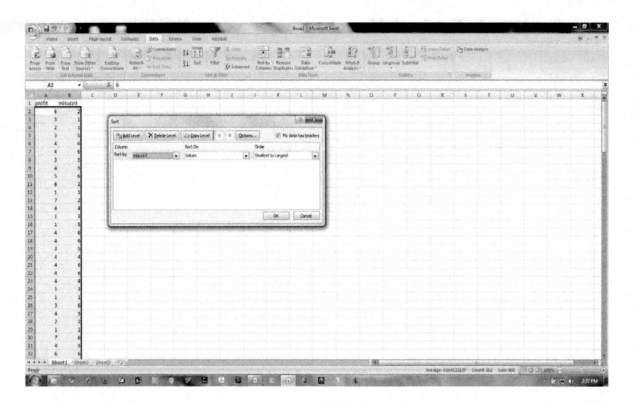

The sorted data in columns A and B are now reformatted into six columns as portrayed in the following screen shot.

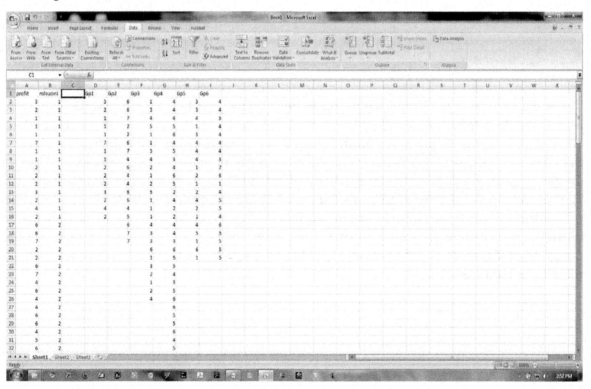

To perform the *ANOVA Single Factor* in Excel, the researcher clicks on *Data Analysis* window. Locate and click on *ANOVA Single Factor*, as noted below, and then click *OK*.

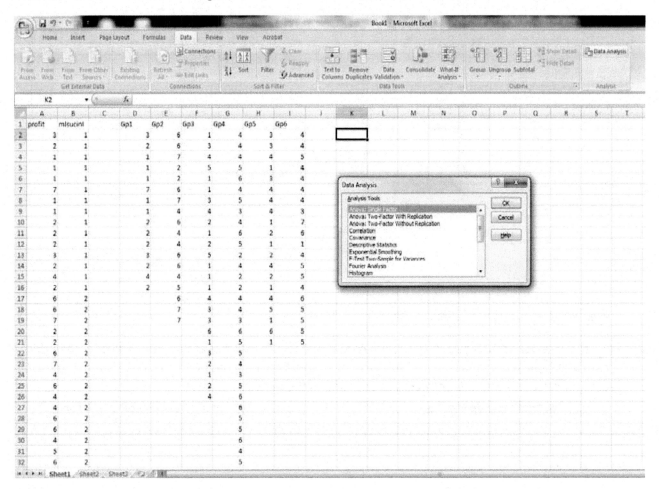

The data that has been reorganized to be analyzed in Excel need to be selected to perform the ANOVA function. In the following screen, the researcher clicks on the Excel icon to right-hand side of the Input Range text box to arrive at a reduced Input Range text box. In this dialog box, assure that the Labels in first row check box is selected, the Grouped by columns radio button is selected, and that Alpha is set to 0.05 unless another value is appropriate.

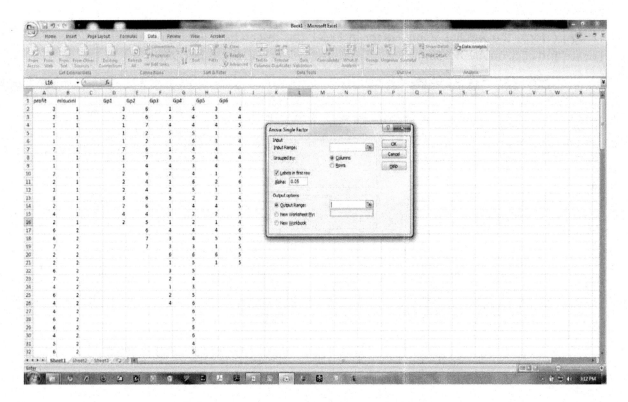

The researcher then selects the entire data range which includes the six columns of data in this case that represents the scaled variable of interest (**profit**) which has been grouped by the nominal/categorical factor variable (**mlsucinl**) as depicted in the next screen shot.

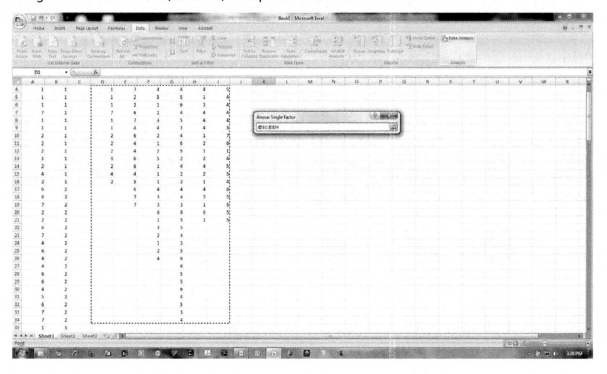

The researcher can now click on the Excel icon at the right-hand side of the reduced text box to return to the *ANOVA Single Factor* dialog box to determine the location of the ANOVA output.

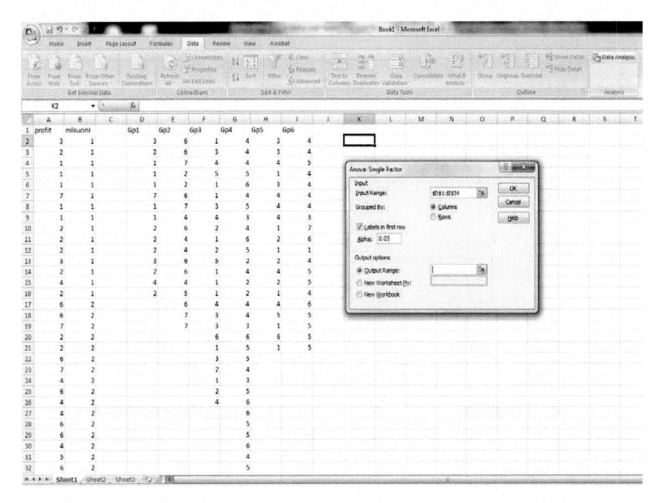

The researcher should next click on the *Output Range* radio button and select the cell, which is cell K2 in this case, that represents the upper left-hand corner of the output results of the ANOVA test being executed.

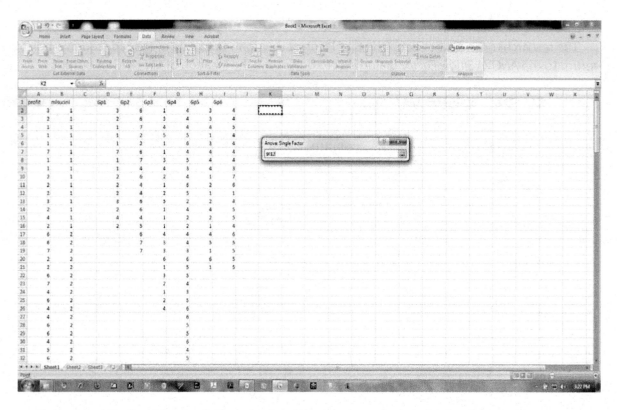

The researcher should next click on the Excel icon at the right-hand side of the reduced text box to return to the *ANOVA Single Factor* dialog box. When this is accomplished, the researcher needs to click *OK*. The following screen shot depicts the results of the *ANOVA Single Factor* test.

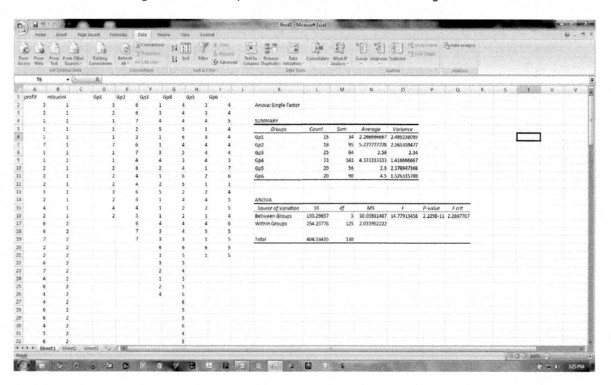

Findings Using Analysis of Variance:

- μ_1 = mean ***profit*** associated with a least success new product from industry #1; μ_2 = mean ***profit*** associated with a most success new product from industry #1; μ_3 = mean ***profit*** associated with a least success new product from industry #2; μ_4 = mean ***profit*** associated with a most success new product from industry #2; μ_5 = mean ***profit*** associated with a least success new product from industry #3; and μ_6 = mean ***profit*** associated with a most success new product from industry #3.

- H_0: $\mu_1 = \mu_2 = \mu_3 = \mu_4 = \mu_5 = \mu_6$ represents the six sample means of the variable distributions.

- The calculated ***F*** statistic is 14.779; the associated ***p*** value is 0.000; To assess the above hypothesis, the researcher uses the ***p*** value of 0.000 noted in the output and an α of 0.05. In this instance, the null hypothesis would be rejected. This suggests that not all of the means tested are equal. Next, the researcher can use the Duncan Post Hoc test to determine which means are not equal.

- The Duncan Post Hoc test lets the researcher know that there are three significant groups of products as they relate to the profits that they earned. The first group comprises the mean ***profit*** associated with a least successful new product from industry #1, the mean ***profit*** associated with a least successful new product from industry #2, and the mean ***profit*** associated with a least successful new product from industry #3.

- The second group contains the mean ***profit*** associated with a most successful new product from industry #2 and the mean ***profit*** associated with a most successful new product from industry #3. It must be noted that groups #2 and #3 overlap with the mean ***profit*** associated with a most successful new product from industry #3 being members of both groups #2 and #3.

- Therefore, the third group contains the mean ***profit*** associated with a most successful new product from industry #3 and the mean ***profit*** associated with a most successful new product from industry #2.

Implications of Research Using Analysis of Variance:

From this test the researcher has determined that the products that are thought to be most successful are produced by industry #2 in this data set. The researcher also determined that the profit means of the three groups of new products from the three industries thought to be least successful were found to be equivalent.

E. Cross Tabulations

Cross tabulations processes are characterized by tables of numbers that can provide significant insight into the information contained in non-monotonic associations between nominal/categorical variables. Cross tabulation tables often provide not only the overall count of responses to each of two variables but also a detailed depiction of the counts of each subgroup of data formed by the intersection of the two variables. Therefore, if one variable is formed by two subgroups such as gender (male and female) and another subgroup is formed by a five point scale (1=low intention to purchase to 5=high intention to purchase) representing a person's intention to purchase a new product, a cross tabulation of these two variables would comprise a table with ten cells. Within each cell would be found the counts representing the number of times respondents selected a particular degree of purchase intent and a particular gender category. What are known as side or marginal totals, percentages, and counts can be calculated. Such figures provide a more refined picture of the number of males that responded as well as the number of total respondents who selected an intention of 1 or a low intention to purchase for example. Additionally in this example, a cell pertaining to Females in the table can provide a more detailed depiction of the data including how many females indicated a high intention to purchase a product or selected 5 on the intention to purchase scale.

A visual inspection of a cross tabulation table can provide the researcher with a picture of what we have called a non-monotonic relationship or lack of non-monotonic relationship between the two variables. This indicates that the two variables might exhibit a relationship with one another but that such a relationship does not indicate that when one variable changes in a particular direction the other variable continuously changes in any particular direction. In other words, the relationship between the two variables will not form a constantly decreasing or increasing function. Moreover, a visual inspection of a cross tabulation table does not provide a researcher with a statistical test that suggests whether a non-monotonic relationship is statistically significant.

F. χ^2-Statistic-Testing for Associations

In chapter 1, the Chi Square (χ^2) distribution and its associated statistic were briefly discussed. The Chi Square statistic can be employed to test whether one nominal/categorical variable is significantly associated with another nominal/categorical variable. In other words, a Chi Square test of the relationship between two variables described by a cross tabulation table can provide a researcher with information regarding the significance of the association between the two variables. The SPSS and Excel exhibits that follow will demonstrate how this is accomplished.

The Chi Square (χ^2) Statistic provides researchers a way to test hypotheses regarding non-monotonic relationships. The null and alternative hypotheses are:

H_0: No Association or non-monotonic relationship between variables

H_A: There exists a significant non-monotonic relationship between variables

a. χ^2 and Cross Tabulation examples and problems to be solved

- χ^2 and cross tabulations can be used to analyze two nominal/categorical variables such as gender and yearly income to determine whether there is a non-monotonic relationship between these two variables.

- χ^2 and cross tabulations can be used to analyze pairs of nominal/categorical variables such as educational level and various forms of advertising media to ascertain whether there is a non-monotonic relationship between the two variables and from what media individuals with higher levels of education obtain information regarding particular products.

- χ^2 and cross tabulations can be used to analyze pairs of nominal/categorical variables such as individuals' intentions to purchase new products and their income levels to determine whether there is a non-monotonic relationship between the two variables and the degree to which purchase intention might represent new product demand based on the individual's ability to make product purchases.

The following SPSS screen shots, diagrams, and statistical outputs depict how a researcher can analyze data using one sample cross tabulation of data based on a χ^2 statistic. The first set of screen shots depicts how one would analyze nominal/categorical variables using the SPSS *Descriptive Statistics* function and *Cross Tabulations*. To arrive at the SPSS screen shot below, click on *Analyze* on the menu bar and then click on *Descriptive Statistics* on the first drop-down menu.

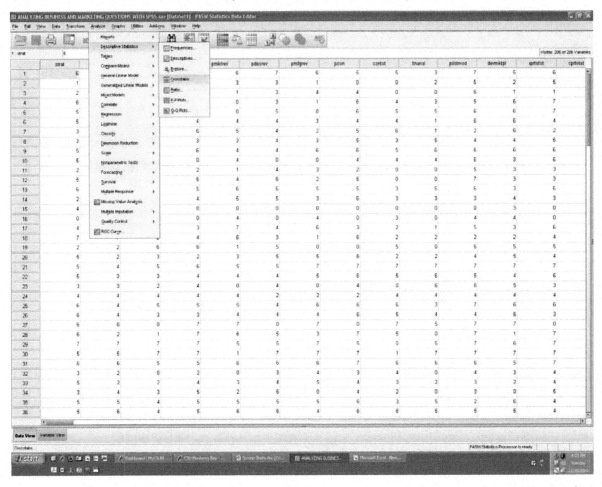

Next the researcher selects the two nominal/categorical variables to be investigated. One variable's data will form the rows of a cross tabulation table and the other variable's data will form the columns of a cross tabulation table. In this instance, the variable **innovati** (the degree of innovativeness of a new product based on a seven point scale where 1=low innovativeness and 7=high innovativeness) forms the rows of the table and the variable **morl** (nominal/categorical data that represent the categories in which the most successful [value =8] and least successful [value=7] products that comprise the units of analysis in a new product development study.) forms the columns of the table. Therefore, the researcher needs to move the variable **innovati** from the window on the right-hand side of the Crosstabs dialog box to the row(s) window on the right-hand side of the Crosstabs dialog box. Then, as SPSS points out, the **innovati** variable is a scaled variable which in this case is interval data. However, since the interval data is represented by a 7-point scale, this variable can also be thought of as a nominal/categorical variable which it is in this example.

Next the researcher should click on the *Cells* button. The *Crosstabs: Cell Display* opens next. In this dialog box, the researcher can select from a variety of options. As noted below, the check boxes for the *Observed* and *Expected* frequency counts are checked. A researcher can also request row, column, and total percentages in this dialog box. A researcher needs to be aware that when several options are requested a cross tabulation printout can become quite large and potentially unmanageable. The researcher should now click the *Continue* button to close the *Crosstabs: Cell Display* dialog box.

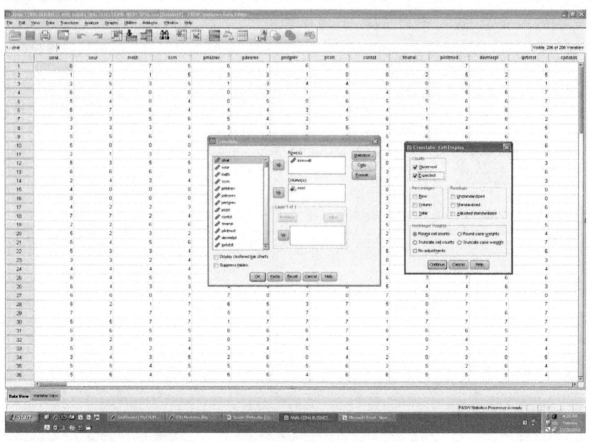

While the *Crosstabs* dialog box is still open, the researcher should click on the *Statistics* button. When the *Statistics* dialog box opens, the researcher needs to select the Chi Square (χ^2) check box and then click *Continue* to return to the *Crosstabs* dialog box in which the researcher now needs to click *OK*.

```
CROSSTABS
  /TABLES=innovati BY morl
  /FORMAT=AVALUE TABLES
  /STATISTICS=CHISQ
  /CELLS=COUNT EXPECTED
  /COUNT ROUND CELL.
```

Crosstabs

[DataSet1] C:\Documents and Settings\mill6391\Desktop\MyStuff\Research\Dissert ation Data\MurrayScaledDissDataSPSS-11-29-2010.sav

Case Processing Summary

	Cases					
	Valid		Missing		Total	
	N	Percent	N	Percent	N	Percent
innovati * morl	131	100.0%	0	.0%	131	100.0%

innovati * morl Crosstabulation

			morl		Total
			7	8	
innovati	1	Count	3	2	5
		Expected Count	2.3	2.7	5.0
	2	Count	6	2	8
		Expected Count	3.6	4.4	8.0
	3	Count	12	4	16
		Expected Count	7.2	8.8	16.0
	4	Count	16	14	30
		Expected Count	13.5	16.5	30.0
	5	Count	10	18	28
		Expected Count	12.6	15.4	28.0
	6	Count	5	18	23
		Expected Count	10.4	12.6	23.0

innovati * morl Crosstabulation

			morl		
			7	8	Total
innovati	7	Count	7	14	21
		Expected Count	9.5	11.5	21.0
Total		Count	59	72	131
		Expected Count	59.0	72.0	131.0

Chi-Square Tests

	Value	df	Asymp. Sig. (2-sided)
Pearson Chi-Square	17.179[a]	6	.009
Likelihood Ratio	17.818	6	.007
Linear-by-Linear Association	12.474	1	.000
N of Valid Cases	131		

a. 4 cells (28.6%) have expected count less than 5. The minimum expected count is 2.25.

The following Excel screen shots, diagrams, and statistical outputs depict how a researcher can create a *pivot table* so that he or she can eventually analyze data using a Chi Square (χ^2) test. The same data employed in the SPSS example will be used to create a pivot table. Therefore, the data pertaining to the variables of interest need to be situated on an Excel spreadsheet as noted in the following screen shot.

Next the researcher chooses two nominal/categorical variables to be investigated which are the same ones employed earlier. One variable's data will form the rows of a pivot table and the other variable's data will form the columns of a pivot table. In this instance, the variable ***innovati*** (the degree of innovativeness of a new product based on a seven point scale where 1=low innovativeness and 7=high innovativeness) forms the rows of the table and the variable ***morl*** (nominal/categorical data that represent the categories in which the most successful [value =8] and least successful [value=7] products that comprise the units of analysis in a new product development study.) forms the columns of the table.

To create a pivot table in Excel, the researcher needs to place the data in the spreadsheet in the appropriate configuration. The next, screen shot depicts the two variables of interest situated next to one another. To begin, the researcher should select an Excel cell which provides an anchor point that can be used to align the upper left-hand corner of the pivot table. In this case, the D3 cell has been selected. Then, in the *Insert* window, locate and click on the *Pivot Table* button on the left-hand side of the *Insert* menu bar. When the *Create Pivot Table* dialog box is opened, the *Existing Worksheet Location* text box will be filled with *Sheet1!D3* which is the D3 cell location.

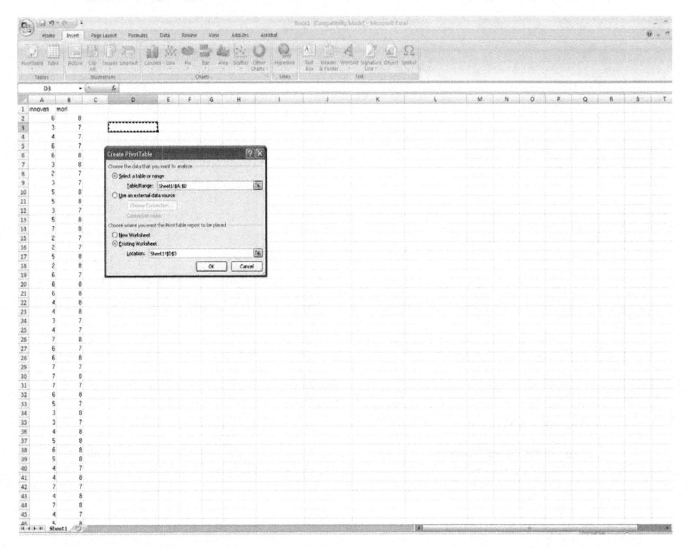

Next the researcher needs to click on the Excel icon on the right-hand side of the *Create Pivot Table: Table/Range* text box to arrive at the following screen shot. In this reduced window, the researcher should select the two columns of data and click on the Excel icon on the right-hand side of the reduced *Create Pivot Table* text box.

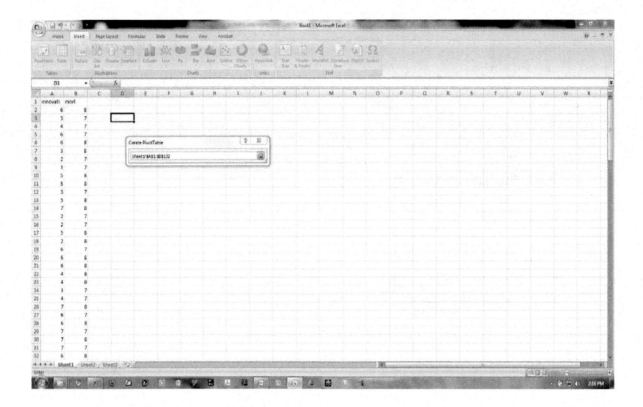

To proceed, the researcher now clicks on the Excel icon on the right-hand side of the reduced *Create Pivot Table* text box to return to the full *Create Pivot Table* text box noted below.

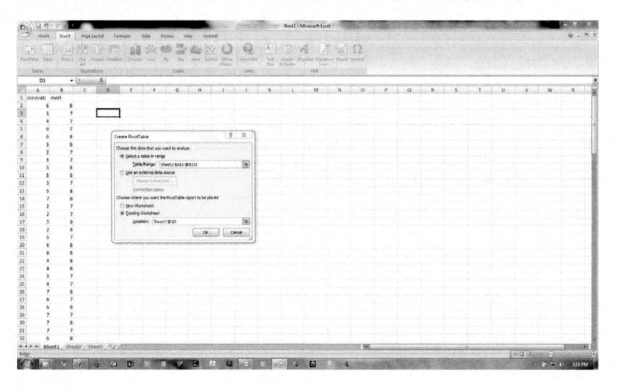

Now click *OK* to display the next screen shot.

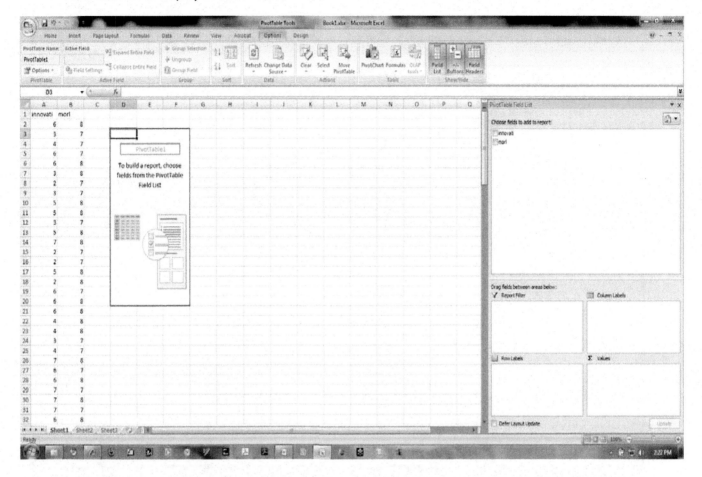

To continue to develop a pivot table similar to the cross tabulation table employed in SPSS, click on ***morl*** in the Pivot Table Field List on the right-hand side of the Excel spreadsheet and drag it to the *Column Labels* box below. Next, click on ***innovati*** and drag it to the *Row Labels* box below. If the Σ Values box in the lower right-hand corner of the *Pivot Table field List* reads *SUM OF MORL*, click on the *SUM OF MORL* link in the *Pivot Table field List* and then click on *Value Field Settings* to change *Sum of MORL* to *Count of MORL*. These steps will yield the following ***morl*** count based pivot table.

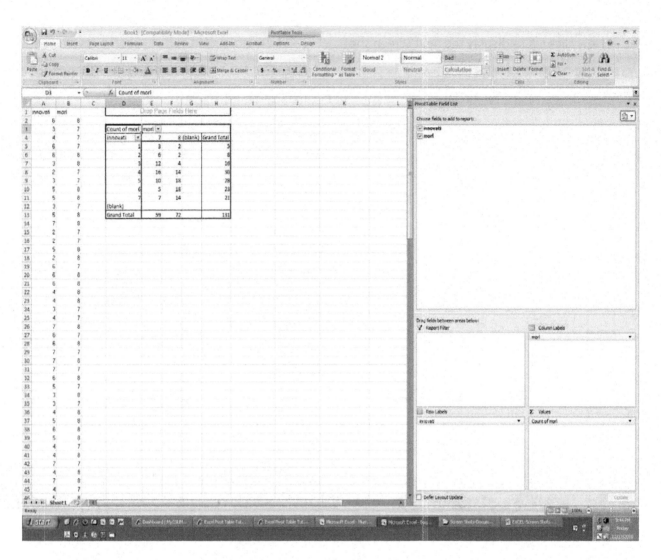

Now that the researcher has developed a pivot table or cross tabulation table, the researcher needs to calculate the expected values for the cross tabulations table. The researcher needs to calculate the expected values that are related to the observed values in the screen shot above. The formula for an expected value is:

Expected Value of a Particular Cell = (Column Total * Row Total) / Grand Total

ie. Expected Value for $Column_1$ & Row_1 = (59 * 5) / 131 = 2.2519

The Expected Values associated with the Observed Values for this example can be found in the table with the upper left-hand corner in the cell E20 in the screen shot below.

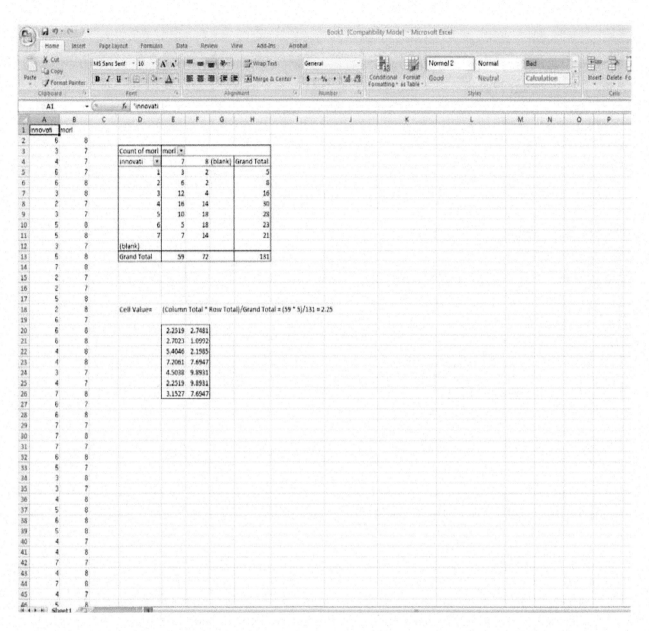

From the *Observed Values* and the calculated *Expected Values*, the researcher can calculate a Chi Square Statistic from the following formula or the CHITEST described below.

Chi Square Statistic (χ^2) = Σ [(Observed Value$_1$ – Expected Value$_1$)^2 / Expected Value$_1$]

To perform the Chi Square calculations using the Excel statistical functions, the researcher needs to perform the CHITEST function. Start the Chi Square Test process by selecting Excel spreadsheet cell F29 as noted below.

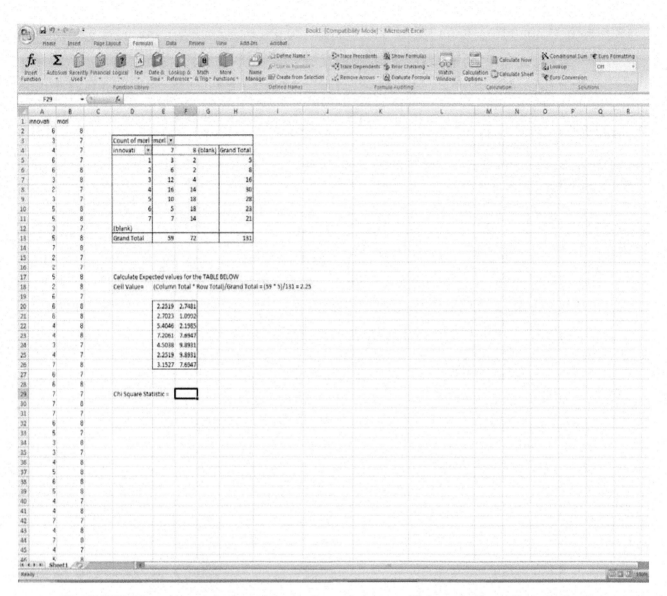

The CHITEST function can be found on the *Formulas* menu. Click on the *Insert Function* button on the left-hand side of the *Formulas* menu. On the *Insert Function* dialog box, locate *Statistical* in the dropdown menu box at the *Or Select a Category* box. Then, in the function selection box below the *Or Select a Category* box select CHITEST. Then click *OK* in the Insert Function dialog box as noted in the following screen shot.

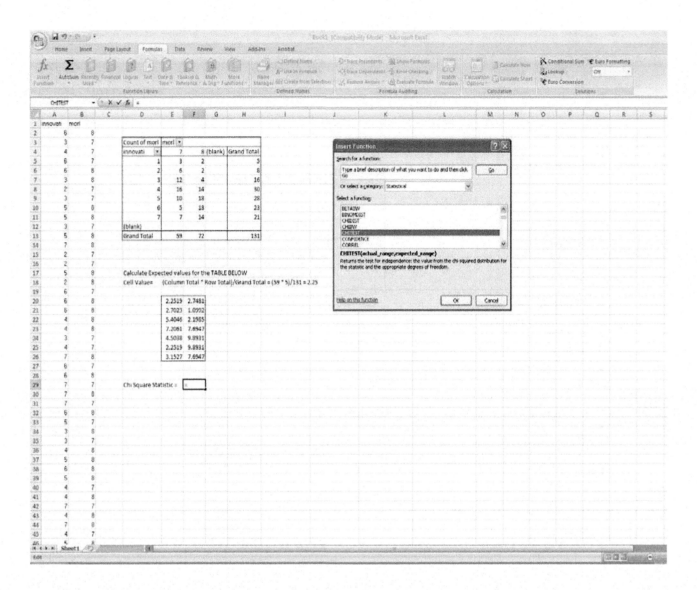

Next the researcher needs to select both columns of the *observed values* by clicking on the Excel icon to the right-hand side of the *Actual Range* text box and then selecting the 14 items in the original pivot table. Then, the researcher needs to click on the Excel icon on the right-hand side of the reduced *Function Arguments* dialog box to return to the primary *Function Arguments* dialog box which is shown below.

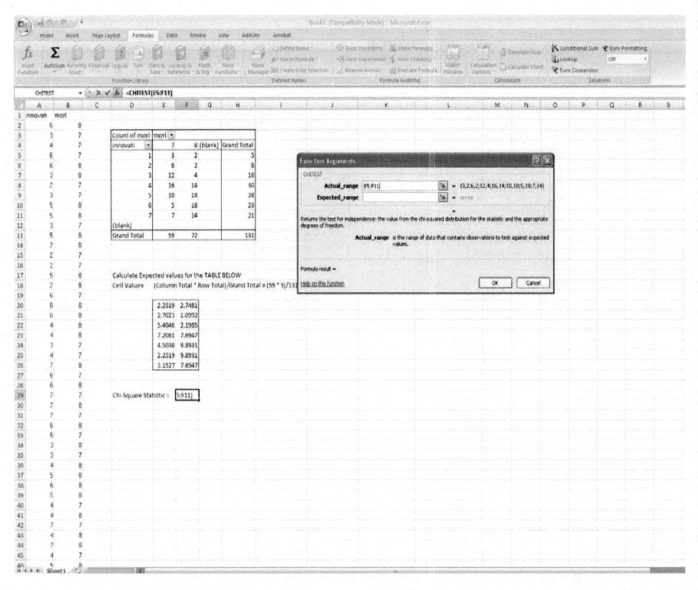

The researcher now needs to select both columns of the *expected values* by clicking on the Excel icon to the right-hand side of the *Expected Range* text box and then selecting the 14 items in the table containing the expected values that were calculated by the researcher. Then, the researcher needs to click on the Excel icon on the right-hand side of the reduced *Function Arguments* dialog box to return to the primary *Function Arguments* dialog box which is shown below.

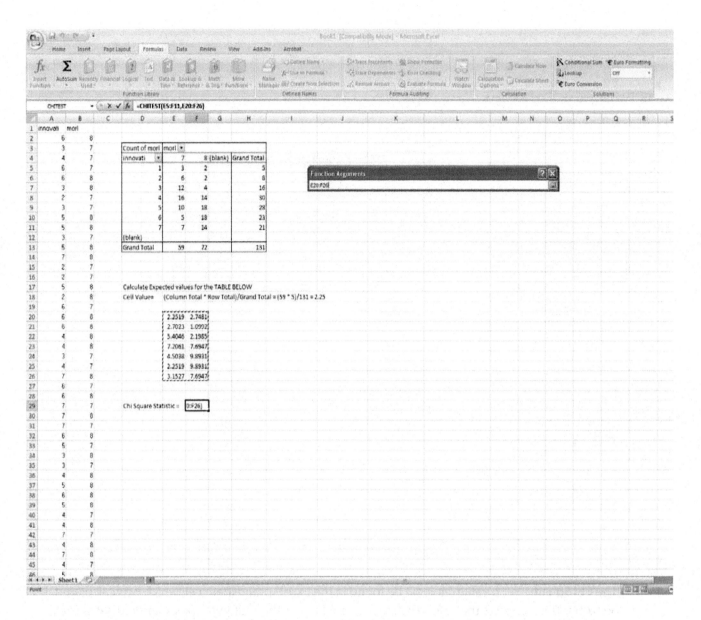

Once the *Observed Value ranges* and the *expected value ranges* have been selected, click *OK* in the *Function Arguments* dialog box.

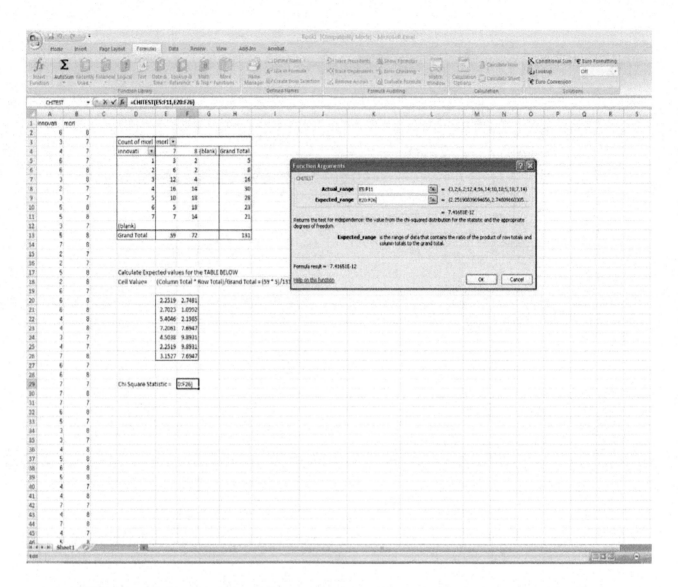

The Chi Square (χ^2) p value can now be found in the Excel spreadsheet cell which was calculated to be 0.009. This suggests that the researcher should reject the null hypothesis and indicates that there is an Association or non-monotonic relationship between the two variables.

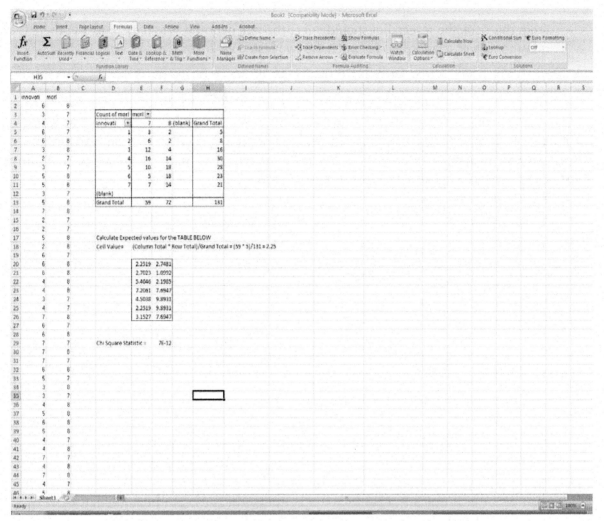

Findings Using Cross Tabulations:

- In this case, the researcher is trying to determine whether there is a non-monotonic relationship between *morl*, which is a categorical variable that represents the most and least successful new products under investigation in this sample, and *innovati*, which is an interval variable that represents the degree of innovativeness perceived by the respondents to this survey process. Since the *innovati* is represented by a 7 point scale, it can be thought of as a nominal variable with 7 categories. To achieve this, the researcher performed a Cross Tabulation and tested the resulting relationship using a Chi Square test.
- The researcher tested the following set of hypotheses in the previous examples.
    - H_0: No Association or non-monotonic relationship between variables
    - H_A: There exists a significant non-monotonic relationship between variables
- The Chi Square (χ^2) statistic is 17.179 and the associated *p* value is 0.009.
- The researcher should employ an $\alpha = 0.05$ unless there is a compelling reason to use another value.

- From this data, the researcher should reject the null hypothesis and assume that there is a non-monotonic relationship between the two tested variables.

Implications of Research Using Cross Tabulations:

The results of this test imply that the most innovative products are thought to be the most successful in this sample of new products. This can be noticed by the larger count values that are associated with the ***innovati*** scores of 4, 5, 6, and 7 that occur in the ***morl*** column associated with a ***morl*** value of 8 which indicates the most successful products in the sample.

Chapter 3

Correlation and Regression

A. Correlation versus Regression

Correlation analysis suggests that the variables of interest are both random variables. The purpose of *Correlation* analysis is to understand the strength of the relationship between two variables that are often thought to be related in a linear fashion. *Regression* analysis typically suggests that one variable [dependent variable] is regressed on one or more variables [independent variable(s)]. The dependent variable(s) is thought to be a random variable whereas the independent variable(s) can be thought of as treatment variables that are controlled by the researcher. The purpose of *Regression* analysis is to find the best fit of a linear model to a set of data so that in some instances dependent variables can be predicted by one or more predictor, explanatory, or independent variables.

B. Scatter Plots

Scatter plots are graphical depictions of data which present the relationship between a dependent variable and an independent variable in a *Regression* situation or two random variables in a *Correlation* situation. Scatter plots represent a good tool to use to investigate the linearity of a relationship between two variables prior to performing a *Correlation* or *Regression* procedure. Since data relationship linearity is a prerequisite for linear *Regression* or linear *Correlation*, it is important to understand whether this requirement is fulfilled by the data.

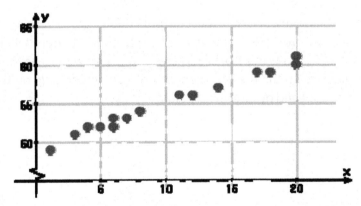

Retrieved from http://www.purplemath.com/modules/scattreg.htm January 14, 2011.

C. Testing Correlations

Correlational relationships can be tested for significance using a *t* test. Statistical software packages such as SPSS often provide *p* values that are associated with either one or two tailed *t* tests for correlations.

The following are hypotheses that are associated with testing the significance of correlation coefficients.

H_0: r = 0; **or** r ≥ 0; **or** r ≤ 0

H_A: r ≠ 0; **or** r < 0; **or** r > 0

The formula:

$$t = r \sqrt{[(n-2)/(1-r)]}$$

where *r* = a correlation coefficient from a sample; *n* = sample size; ρ = rho = a population correlation coefficient

a. Examples and problems to be solved with Correlations

- Correlation analyses can be used to determine the strength of the relationship between the intent to purchase models of the same product category.
- Correlation analyses can be used to investigate the strength of the relationship between number of hours needed to produce a product and the number of units sold.
- Correlation analyses can be used to understand the strength of the relationship between the number of investors in a project and the number of customers of the products developed by the project.

The following SPSS screen shots, diagrams, and statistical outputs depict how a researcher can analyze data using bivariate correlation processes. The first set of screen shots depict how one would analyze scaled (interval or ratio) data using the SPSS *Correlation Function*. To arrive at the SPSS screen shot below, click on *Analyze* on the menu bar and then click on *Correlate* on the first drop-down menu and *Bivariate* on the second drop-down menu.

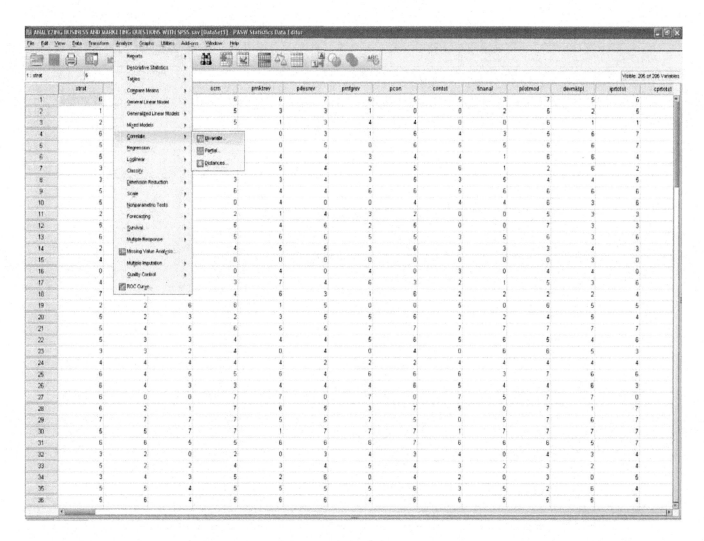

Next select the variables to be investigated from the left window in the *Bivariate Correlations* dialog box. In this case, the ***profit***, ***pdesrev***, ***pmktrev***, and ***pmfgrev*** variables were selected and moved from the left-hand window in the Bivariate Correlations dialog box to the right-hand window in the same dialog box. In this case, the researcher is trying to determine the strength of the relationship between a sample of firms' profits for particular new products and ***pdesrev*** (degree of proficiency with which a preliminary design review was accomplished), ***pmktrev*** (degree of proficiency with which a preliminary marketing review was accomplished), and ***pmfgrev*** (degree of proficiency with which a preliminary manufacturing review was accomplished). These variables were measured using a 7 point interval scale. The profit scale is driven by the statement "This product's profits were *worse/better* than expected" where *worse* is represented by 1 on the scale and *better* is represented by 7.

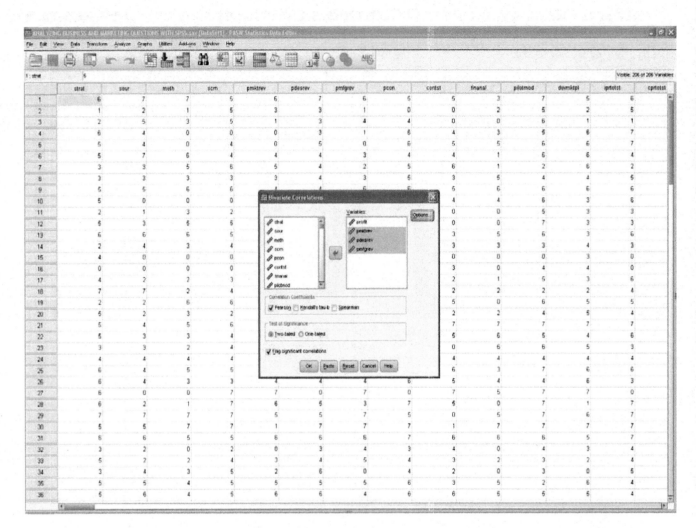

Please note the following to review the SPSS output for a *Bivariate Correlation Test* of ***four pairs of variables***. Note that the depicted correlation coefficients are related to only two variables at a time without any influence or impact from the other variables. In other words, these tests are thought to **not** involve simultaneous tests or involvement with other variables beyond the two variables under investigation..

```
CORRELATIONS
  /VARIABLES=profit pmktrev pdesrev pmfgrev
  /PRINT=TWOTAIL NOSIG
  /MISSING=PAIRWISE.
```

Correlations

[DataSet1] C:\Documents and Settings\mill6391\Desktop\MyStuff\Research\Dissert
ation Data\MurrayScaledDissDataSPSS-8-9-2010.sav

Correlations

		profit	pmktrev	pdesrev	pmfgrev
profit	Pearson Correlation	1	.260	.321	.321
	Sig. (2-tailed)		.003	.000	.000
	N	131	131	131	131
pmktrev	Pearson Correlation	.260	1	.372	.378
	Sig. (2-tailed)	.003		.000	.000
	N	131	131	131	131
pdesrev	Pearson Correlation	.321	.372	1	.416
	Sig. (2-tailed)	.000	.000		.000
	N	131	131	131	131
pmfgrev	Pearson Correlation	.321	.378	.416	1
	Sig. (2-tailed)	.000	.000	.000	
	N	131	131	131	131

**. Correlation is significant at the 0.01 level (2-tailed).

The following Excel screen shots, diagrams, and statistical outputs depict how a researcher can analyze data using *Correlation* procedures in Excel. In this case, the ***profit***, ***pdesrev***, ***pmktrev***, and ***pmfgrev*** variables were selected for study. The data pertaining to the variables of interest need to be situated on an Excel spreadsheet as noted in the following. All of the variables under investigation need two scales (interval or ratio). In this case, the variables to be analyzed were measured using of 7-point Likert scales.

To perform a *Correlation* test in Excel, the researcher needs to place the data in the Excel spreadsheet in the appropriate configuration. The next screen shot depicts how the data might be found when it is input from survey instruments either in paper or electronic form. The researcher needs to click on *Data Analysis* at the right end of the *Data* menu, locate, and click on *Correlation*, as noted below, and then click *OK*.

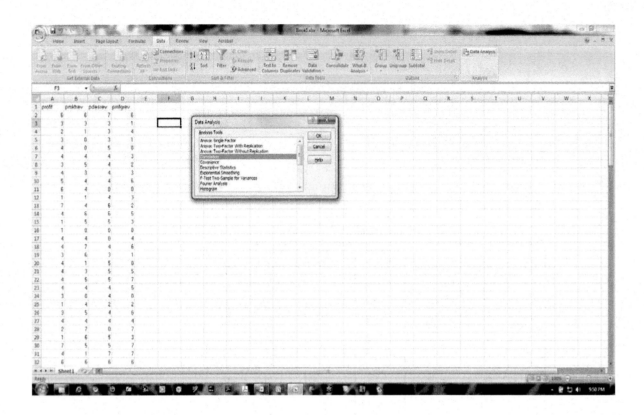

In the *Correlation* dialog box, click on the Excel icon at the right-hand side of the *Input Range* text box.

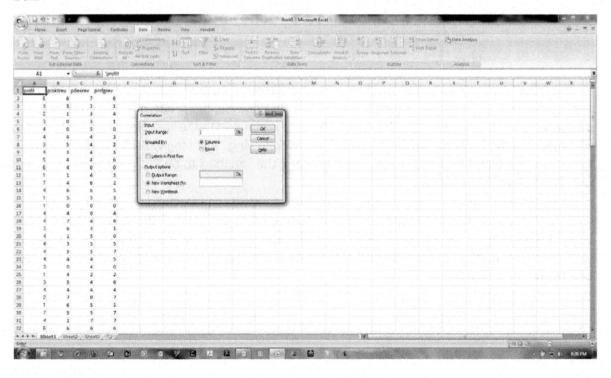

Select all four columns of data to provide the input for the reduced *Input Range* text box depicted in the following screen shot. Then, click on the Excel icon at the right-hand side of the *Output Range* and select the spreadsheet cell in this case G8 which represents the upper left-hand corner of the *Correlation* output results as noted in the next screen shot.

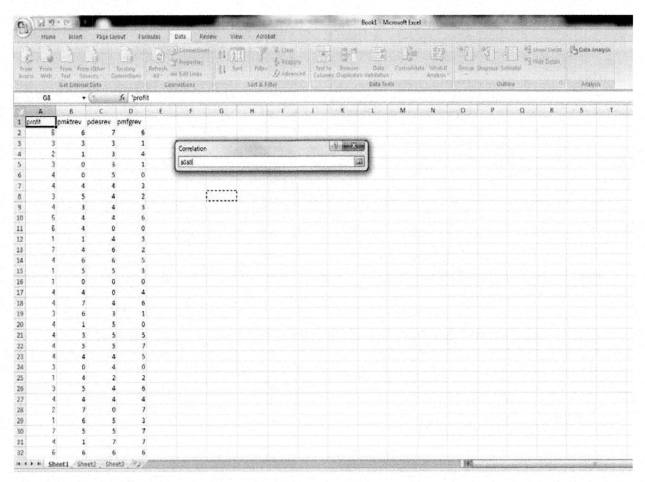

Click on the Excel icon to the right-hand side of the reduced *Correlation* dialog box to return to the *Correlation* dialog box.

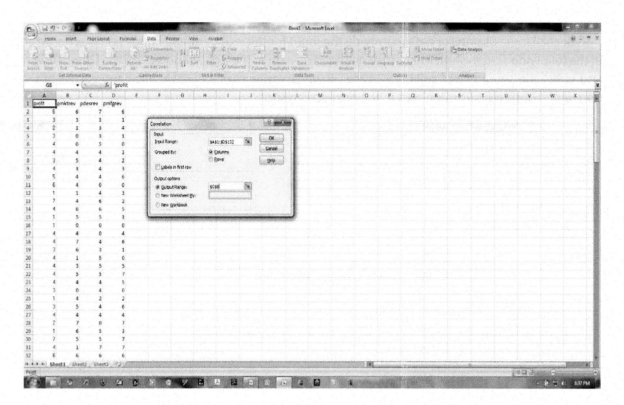

Then the researcher needs to click *OK* to produce the output from the *Correlation* analysis.

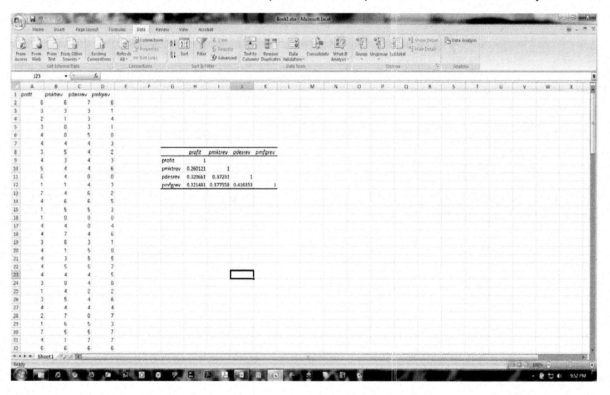

	profit	pmktrev	pdesrev	pmfgrev
profit	1			
pmktrev	0.260121	1		
pdesrev	0.320661	0.37231	1	
pmfgrev	0.321481	0.377558	0.416353	1

Findings Using Correlations:

- In this instance, the researcher is trying to determine whether there is a relationship between **profit**, which is a scaled variable that represents the perceived profit of the new products under investigation in this research, and **pmktrev**, **pdesrev**, and **pmfgrev** which represent the perceived degrees of proficiency with which the marketing, design, and manufacturing review processes are performed as perceived by the respondents to this survey process. All of the three review variables were measured using 7 point, interval scales. It is therefore appropriate for the researcher to use the Correlations process to determine the possible relationships among these four variables.
- The researcher tested the following set of hypotheses in the previous examples.

   $H_0: \rho = 0$; $H_A: \rho \neq 0$; these hypotheses were tested to determine whether there is a statistically significant relationship among these variables but not whether the re-lationships might be direct or inverse. The signs of the correlation coefficients will inform the researcher whether the relationships are direct or inverse.

- The researcher should employ an $\alpha = 0.05$ unless there is a compelling reason to use another value.
- The correlation coefficients are 0.280, 0.321 (which occurred twice), 0.372, 0.378, and 0.418. All of these correlation coefficients are positive indicating direct relationships between each pair or variables. The p values ranged from 0.000 to 0.003. These p values are much less than the α of 0.05 which suggests to the researcher that he/she should reject the null hypotheses that the correlation coefficients are zero.

Implications of Research Using Correlations:

It must be remembered that these correlation coefficients were calculated with reference to only two variables at a time with no relationship to the other variables. The results of this test imply that perceived profit is significantly correlated with the proficiency with which all three of the tested new product review processes are performed. The largest correlation was found to be with the proficiency with which the design review and manufacturing review processes were performed as opposed to the proficiency with which the marketing review process was performed. However, it must be remembered that the correlation between perceived profit and the proficiency with which the marketing review process is performed is also quite significant. Therefore, the interpretation of the results of this test should suggest that the proficiency with which all of the review processes are performed is important to the perceived profit of new products.

D. Creating Regression Models

Regression models can be created for two major purposes which predict the dependent variable(s) and/or characterize the primary independent variables that impact the dependent variable(s). *Regression* models need to be developed with theory in mind. The selected independent variables need to be chosen with consideration for their potential relationship with the dependent variable under consideration. *Regression* models can be formed by a minimum of two variables which include one dependent variable and one independent variable. *Regression* models can also include multiple independent as well as multiple dependent variables (not discussed in this volume). *Regression* models most often include variables that have been measured using either interval or ratio data however nominal/categorical variables can also be incorporated in *Regression* models.

E. Specify, Formulate/Fit, and Diagnose a Model

First, a researcher needs to specify a *Regression* Model which requires the researcher to determine dependent and independent variables, a population of interest as in many other research processes, and settle on a sampling process to gather data to develop a *Regression* model.

Second, the researcher should investigate the aptness of the regression model as detailed next in paragraph F of this chapter.

Third, a researcher needs to formulate hypotheses to determine whether the overall *Regression* model is significant as described further in paragraph H below.

Fourth, the researcher ought to examine the *Coefficient of Determination* and the *Adjusted Coefficient of Determination* as discussed in paragraph G below to establish the degree of variation in the dependent variable that is explained by the selected independent variables.

Fifth, the researcher should evaluate the *F* statistic and its associated *p* value to ascertain whether the null hypothesis described in paragraph H below can be rejected and the Regression model can be used.

Sixth, if the *Regression* model is significant and the *Regression* model is a *Multiple Regression* model, the researcher needs to evaluate the hypotheses related to the significance of each of the individual independent variables as discussed in paragraph H below.

Seventh, at the end of this chapter, additional issues are discussed that the researcher needs to explore that include multicollinearity, which occurs when independent variables are highly correlated, and the scope of the model, which describes the range of the X variable(s) to which the model applies..

F. Aptness of a Regression Model-Study the Data

Researchers need to pay special attention to their gathered data to be sure that the data is appropriate to be analyzed and modeled using linear Regression.

a. The Regression function is linear in the parameters

Scatter plots, as discussed earlier, can be used to investigate from a graphical perspective the visual characteristics of the data to ascertain whether it might demonstrate linear characteristics. The following scatter plot that relates an individual's shoe size to age appears to form a relatively linear function. If linearity is not apparent, a researcher must either transform the data (this topic is not more fully addressed here) or assume that a linear regression model is not appropriate. The data depicted in the scatter plot below appears to suggest that the variables in the portrayed relationship are linearly related.

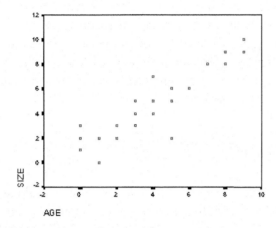

Retrieved from http://www.ltcconline.net/greenl/courses/201/regression/scatter.htm
January 15, 2011

b. Constant Variance of Error Terms

The differences between each **y** measurement and a calculated regression line, or error terms need to exhibit a constant variance. Constant variance is also known as homoscedasticity over the range of predicted values.

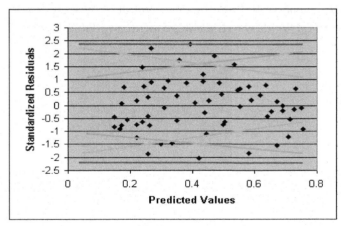

Retrieved from http://mallit.fr.umn.edu/fr4218/assigns/excel_reg.html and modified
January 15, 2011

The distribution of Standardized Residuals over the values predicted by the Regression Model appears to depict a relatively **constant** variation about 0.0 over the range of the Predicted Values as demonstrated by the RED lines on the chart above. Had the distribution of Standardized Residuals across the Predicted Values aligned with the BLUE or GREEN lines, the researcher would have to assume that there exists a confounding factor that is influencing the noted residual trend.

c. Normally Distributed Error Terms

A researcher needs to evaluate the degree to which the regression error terms are normally distributed. This process does not evaluate the normality of the raw data measures. Its focus is on the error terms which are created by the degree of differentiation between the observed data and the calculated regression line. There are several tests for normality that can be employed. One of these normality tests is the *Shapiro-Wilk* test which is recommended for small to medium sized samples where $n \leq 2000$. The hypotheses to test normality of error terms are:

H_0: The error terms are normally distributed

H_A: The error terms are not normally distributed

If the *Shapiro-Wilk* test statistic associated *p* value is less than 0.05, a researcher should reject the null hypothesis that the error terms are normally distributed. In order to ascertain the normality of regression error terms, the standardized residuals must be calculated and saved as a separate SPSS variable. Values for regression error terms can be calculated in SPSS by employing the following process after executing the regression function which is described more fully later in this chapter. The error terms need to be saved in SPSS by clicking on *Analyze* then Regression then Linear to arrive at the *Linear Regression* window. In the *Linear Regression* window, the researcher needs to move a dependent variable such as **longrgth** (a respondent's perception that there will be long-range new product growth) from the left-hand window in the *Linear Regression* window to the *Dependent* variable text box and an independent variable such as **resourcs** (the degree to which a respondent perceives that there will be resources available to fund the develpment of new products) from the left-hand window in the *Linear Regression* window to the *Independent(s)* variable text box.

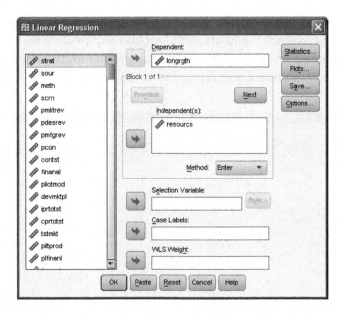

The researcher then needs to click on the *Save* button and complete other steps relative to the Regression function also described later in this chapter. The *Linear Regression: Save* dialog box will open. In the *Linear Regression: Save* dialog box, the researcher needs to check the box next to *Standardized* in the *Residuals* area of the *Linear Regression: Save* dialog box as noted below and then click *Continue*.

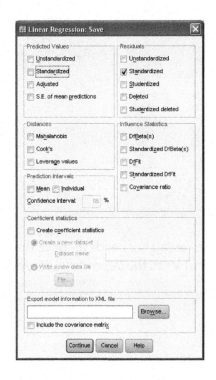

Next the researcher needs to click **Continue** to return to the Linear Regression dialog box and then click OK. This action will run the Regression function and create a variable called ZRE_1 which represents the *Standardized Residuals* of the tested *Regression* function. Next the researcher needs to click *Analyze, Descriptive Statistics*, and *Explore* as noted below.

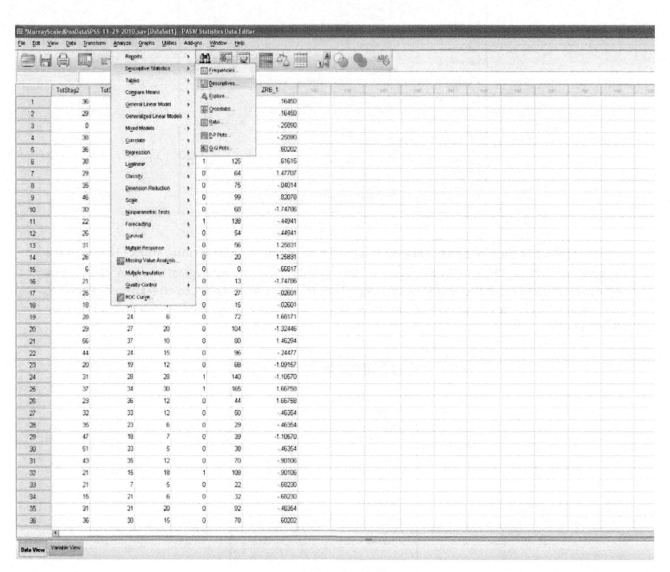

In the Explore dialog box, the researcher needs to move the ZRE_1 (*Standardized Residual*) variable from the left-hand list of variables to the *Dependent List* text box. Next, click on the *Plots* button.

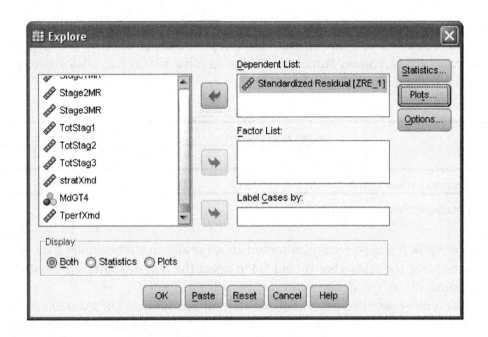

This action will take the researcher to the *Explore: Plots* dialog box.

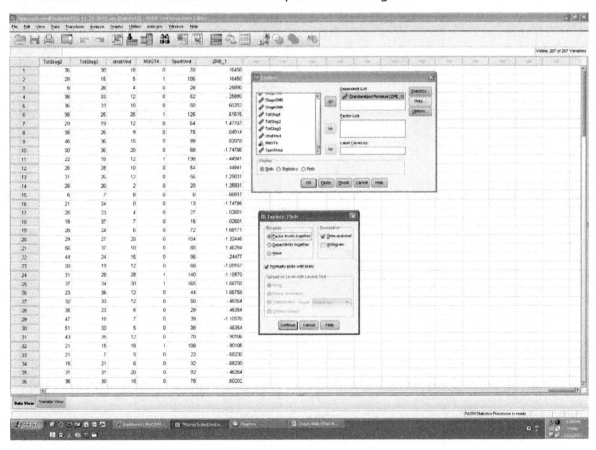

Be sure that the *Normality plots with tests* check box is selected (the Stem and Leaf check box need not be selected) and click *Continue* to return to the *Explore* dialog box. Next click *OK* to perform the *Explore* function. The following output in addition to other results (*Case Processing Summary* and *Descriptives*) will be presented.

Tests of Normality

	Kolmogorov-Smirnov[a]			Shapiro-Wilk		
	Statistic	df	Sig.	Statistic	df	Sig.
Standardized Residual	.083	131	.028	.985	131	.169

a. Lilliefors Significance Correction

The *Shapiro-Wilk Test of Normality* presented above results in a **p** or significance value of 0.169, which suggests that the researcher should fail to reject the null hypothesis presented earlier and that the residuals of the tested regression are normally distributed.

A Q-Q Plot is also presented as a visual depiction of the normality of a variable, in this case the residuals of a regression process. The closer the values, depicted in the following graph as circles, are to the straight line, the more likely the variable or residuals are to be normally distributed.

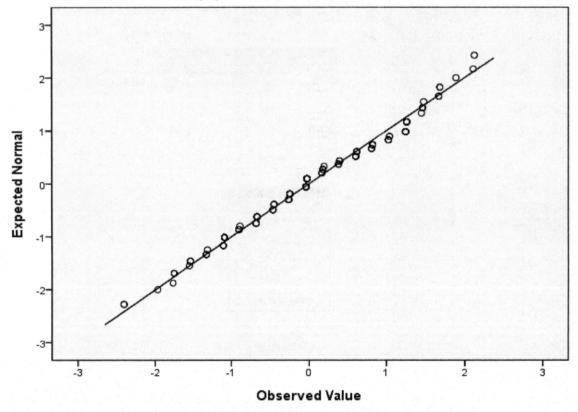

Normal Q-Q Plot of Standardized Residual

d. Independent Error Terms especially for Time Series Models

For time series regression models, researchers need to assure that the error terms are not varying with time or other independent variables. An implication is that subsequent measures in time are influenced by preceding measures. A Durbin-Watson test statistic (d) can be calculated to assess the impact of what are known as autocorrelated residuals and has a range from 0 to 4. Therefore, autocorrelation suggests that error terms are correlated with prior and future error terms. What follows are two sets of hypotheses used to test the independence of error terms.

$H_0: \rho = 0; H_A: \rho > 0$ when $d > d$U, there is no correlation among residual error terms
when $d < d$L, there exists positive autocorrelation in the data

$H_0: \rho = 0; H_A: \rho < 0$ when $(4\text{-}d) > d$U, there is no correlation among residual error terms
when $(4\text{-}d) < d$L, there exists negative autocorrelation in the data

To test for autocorrelation in data, a *Durbin-Watson* test statistic (d) can be calculated using SPSS as noted below. To perform this test, the researcher is led to believe that a new product's perceived profits (**profit**) tend to change in either a positive or negative manner in accordance with the proficiency with which the strategy for new product development processes are performed (**strat**). To perform this test, the researcher clicks on *Analyze*, *Regression*, and *Linear*.

In the *Linear Regression* dialog box, the researcher needs to move the ***pdesrev*** in the left-hand list of variables to the *Dependent* variable text box on the right-hand side of the *Linear Regression* dialog box. Next the researcher needs to move the ***strat*** variable from the left-hand list of variables to the *Independent(s)* variable text box on the right-hand side of the *Linear Regression* dialog box. Now, the researcher should click on the *Statistics* button to open the *Linear Regression: Statistics* dialog box. In the *Linear Regression: Statistics* dialog box, assure that the *Durbin-Watson* check box is selected. Next click *Continue* to return to the *Linear Regression* dialog box and then click *OK* to produce the output of this process.

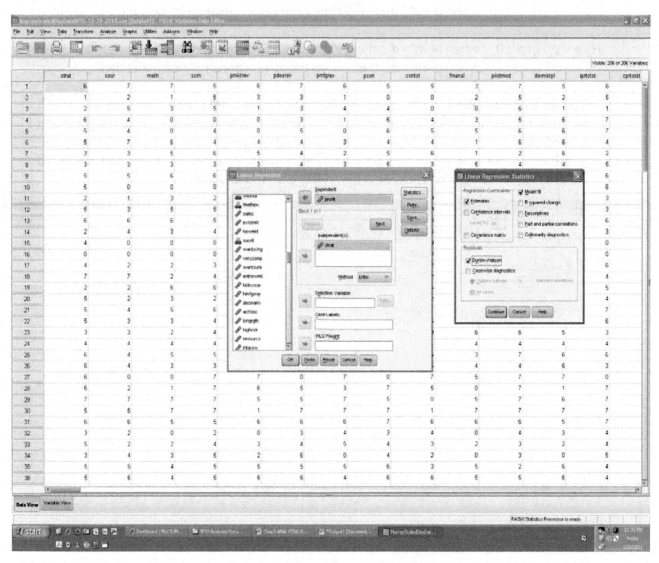

In addition to the typical Model Summary data that will be produced, this process also reveals the *Durbin-Watson* test statistic, which in this instance is 1.938 as noted below. A more detailed discussion of simple and multiple regression follows later in this chapter.

```
GET
  FILE='C:\Documents and Settings\mill6391\Desktop\MyStuff\Research\Dissertati
on Data\MurrayScaledDissDataSPSS-11-29-2010.sav'.
DATASET NAME DataSet1 WINDOW=FRONT.
REGRESSION
  /MISSING LISTWISE
  /STATISTICS COEFF OUTS R ANOVA
  /CRITERIA=PIN(.05) POUT(.10)
  /NOORIGIN
  /DEPENDENT profit
  /METHOD=ENTER strat
  /RESIDUALS DURBIN.
```

Regression

[DataSet1] C:\Documents and Settings\mill6391\Desktop\MyStuff\Research\Dissert
ation Data\MurrayScaledDissDataSPSS-11-29-2010.sav

Variables Entered/Removed[b]

Model	Variables Entered	Variables Removed	Method
1	strat[a]	.	Enter

a. All requested variables entered.

b. Dependent Variable: profit

Model Summary[b]

Model	R	R Square	Adjusted R Square	Std. Error of the Estimate	Durbin-Watson
1	.217[a]	.047	.039	1.735	1.938

a. Predictors: (Constant), strat

b. Dependent Variable: profit

ANOVA[b]

Model		Sum of Squares	df	Mean Square	F	Sig.
1	Regression	18.941	1	18.941	6.295	.013[a]
	Residual	385.128	128	3.009		
	Total	404.069	129			

a. Predictors: (Constant), strat

b. Dependent Variable: profit

Coefficients[a]

Model		Unstandardized Coefficients		Standardized Coefficients	t	Sig.
		B	Std. Error	Beta		
1	(Constant)	2.822	.376		7.504	.000
	strat	.205	.082	.217	2.509	.013

a. Dependent Variable: profit

Residuals Statistics[a]

	Minimum	Maximum	Mean	Std. Deviation	N
Predicted Value	2.82	4.26	3.68	.383	130
Residual	-3.260	4.178	.000	1.728	130
Std. Predicted Value	-2.252	1.501	.000	1.000	130
Std. Residual	-1.879	2.409	.000	.996	130

a. Dependent Variable: profit

A *Durbin-Watson* test statistic (*d*) needs to be compared to upper and lower critical values of the *Durbin-Watson* test statistic. To test for negative autocorrelation, the researcher needs to subtract the *Durbin-Watson* test statistic from 4 and perform the same procedure as would need to be performed when using *d* alone. If the *Durbin-Watson* test statistic (*d* or 4-*d*) is less than the upper (*d*U) and greater than the lower (*d*L) value, the *Durbin-Watson* test is inconclusive. However, if the *Durbin-Watson* test statistic (*d* or 4-*d*) is greater than the upper value (*d*U), the researcher should fail to reject H_0. This suggests that there is either no positive or negative autocorrelation present. If the *Durbin-Watson* test statistic *d* or (4-*d*)is less than the lower value, the researcher should reject H_0 (there is no autocorrelation present either positive or negative).

Therefore, *Durbin Watson* test statistics close to 0 indicate positive autocorrelation whereas *Durbin Watson* test statistics close to 4 suggests negative autocorrelation. *Durbin Watson* test statistics that are approximately 2 indicate no positive or negative, serial correlation.

Employing an α of 0.05 and with a single independent variable included in the model, the applicable *Durbin Watson* tabled measures for a sample size of 100 are (*d*U=1.694; and *d*L=1.654) and for a sample size of 150 are (*d*U=1.747; and *d*L=1.720). Using linear interpolation to arrive at the *Durbin Watson* tabled measures for a sample size of n = 131 yield upper and lower *Durbin Watson* tabled measures of *d*U=1.73674 and *d*L=1.6788. Therefore, a *Durbin Watson* statistic of 1.938 with a sample size of n = 131, which is less than *d*L = 1.6788, suggests that the researcher should fail to reject H_0 and assume that the error terms in this instance exhibit no positive autocorrelation. This suggests that the error terms or residuals are not related to one another. To test for negative autocorrelation, the researcher subtracts *d* = 1.618 from 4 which yields 2.062. When the researcher compares this Durbin Watson test statistic to the Lower and Upper *Durbin Watson* tabled, interpolated test statistics calculated earlier (*d*U=1.73674 and *d*L=1.6788), the researcher notes that the *Durbin Watson* test statistic (4-*d*) is greater than the interpolated, tabled test statistic. Therefore, the researcher should fail to reject the null hypothesis assuming that there is also no negative autocorrelation.

G. Coefficient of Determination-Adjusted Coefficient of determination

The Coefficient of Determination or R^2 is the square of a correlation coefficient. In a *Simple Linear Regression* process the correlation coefficient represents the correlation between the dependent variable and independent variable. The decimal value of R^2 multiplied by 100 represents the percent of the variability in the dependent variable that is explained by the independent variable in *Simple Linear Regression* and the percent of the variability in the dependent variable that is explained simultaneously by all of the independent variables in a *Multiple Linear Regression* process. This metric is important since the magnitude of R^2 suggests whether there are independent variables that are missing from the model and to what extent the missing independent variables might impact dependent variable especially if the formula derived by the *Regression* process is to be used to predict the dependent variable.

As independent variables are added to a *Regression* model, the *Coefficient of Determination* or R^2 always increases to some degree. To determine whether the increase in R^2 is solely due to a new independent variable being added to the *Regression* model or whether the newly added independent variable provides essential increased explanatory power to the *Regression* model. To make this determination, an *Adjusted Coefficient of Determination* metric can be calculated, which is modified by the number of independent variables in the *Regression* model and the sample size (n). The inclusion of the number of independent variables in a *Regression* model and the sample size (n) in the calculation of an *Adjusted Coefficient of Determination* always makes an *Adjusted Coefficient of Determination* less than or equal to the original magnitude of a *Coefficient of Determination*. The equation for the *Adjusted Coefficient of Determination* follows.

$$R^2_{adj} = 1 - (1 - R^2) [(n - 1)/(n - k - 1)]$$
where $\boldsymbol{R^2}$ is the *Coefficient of Determination*, $\boldsymbol{n}$ is the sample size, and $\boldsymbol{k}$ is the number of independent variables in the *Regression* model

It should be noted that R^2_{adj} is always less than 1. Also, $(1 - R^2)$ represents the unexplained portion of the dependent variable. If R^2 had been increased by adding more independent variables to the *Regression* model, then the unexplained portion of the dependent variable would have decreased. It should be noted that the following factor $[(n - 1)/(n - k - 1)]$ always increases the degree of the unexplained portion of a *Regression* process. Therefore, the difference between 1 and a slightly increased unexplained portion of the dependent variable slightly lowers R^2 to R^2_{adj}.

H. F-Statistic and *t* Statistics-Testing a Regression Model

Simple Linear Regression produces an *F* statistic with an associated *p* value to suggest to the researcher whether the null hypothesis can be rejected. If the *p* value associated with the *F* statistic is less than the Alpha that the researcher selects which is typically assigned the value of 0.05, the researcher can reject the null hypothesis. The null and alternative hypotheses associated with *Simple Linear Regression* follow.

H_0: The coefficient of the independent variable $(\boldsymbol{\beta_1}) = 0$

H_A: The coefficient of the independent variable $(\boldsymbol{\beta_1}) \neq 0$

Multiple Linear Regression differs from *Simple Linear Regression* in that *Multiple Linear Regression* involves more than one independent *X* variable whereas *Simple Linear Regression* involves only a single independent *X* variable. *Multiple Linear Regression* also produces an *F* statistic with an associated *p* value to suggest to the researcher whether the null hypothesis can be rejected. If the *p* value associated with the *F* statistic is less than the Alpha that the researcher selects which is typically assigned the value of 0.05, the researcher can reject the null hypothesis. The null and alternative hypotheses associated with *Multiple Linear Regression* follow.

H_0: All of the coefficients of the independent variables $(\boldsymbol{\beta_1, \beta_2, \beta_n}) = 0$

H_A: At least one the coefficients of the independent variables $(\boldsymbol{\beta_1, \beta_2, \beta_n}) \neq 0$

Since there is more than one independent (*X*) variable involved in a *Multiple Linear Regression* process and, when the null hypothesis [H_0: All of the coefficients of the independent variables (β_1, β_2, β_n) = 0] is rejected, the researcher needs to inspect all of the *p* values associated with regression's coefficients or *b* values to ascertain which coefficients or β values are not statistically equal to zero. The *p* value associated with each β needs to be compared to the Alpha that the researcher selects which is typically assigned the value of 0.05. For β values that are associated with *p* values which are less than 0.05, the null hypotheses are individually rejected and it is assumed that those particular independent variables are significantly related to the dependent *Y* variable.

I. Simple Linear Regression

Simple linear regression is a process in which a single dependent variable (*Y*) is regressed on a single independent variable (*X*). The formula in the form of *Y = mx + b* (where *m* is the slope of a straight line and *b* is the intercept of the *Y* axis) which represents this relationship and includes constant and error terms is:

$Y = \beta_0 + \beta_1 X_1 + \varepsilon$ where β_0 the constant term or intercept of the Y axis; β_1 is the slope of a straight line and the coefficient of X_1; and ε is an error term.

The assumptions of the error term are that the error term has a mean of zero, a constant variance, and is not correlated with itself across the errors associated with various observations.

The following SPSS screen shots, diagrams, and statistical outputs depict how a researcher can analyze data using simple linear regression using scaled (interval and/or ratio) data. To arrive at the SPSS screen shot below, click on *Analyze* on the menu bar and then click on *Regression* on the first

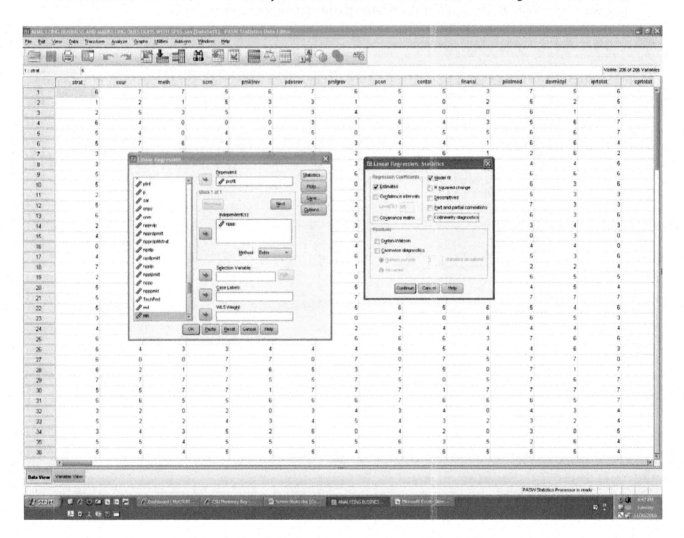

drop-down menu and *Linear* on the second drop-down menu.

For the simple linear regression example, the researcher is regressing **profit** (this is a measure representing the perceived profit from a newly launched product using a scale that is driven by the statement "This product's profits were *worse/better* than expected" where *worse* is represented by

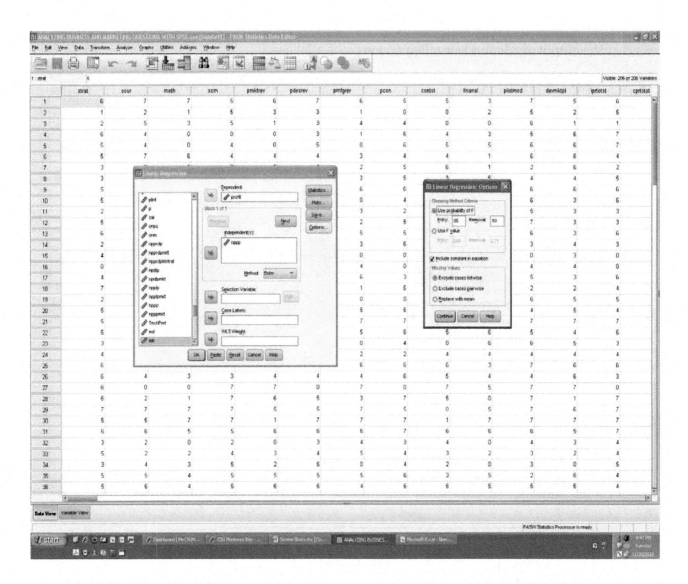

1 on the scale and *better* is represented by 7) on **nppp** (this is a measure of the overall proficiency with which a new product development process is performed measured on a 7-point interval scale).

To perform a Simple Linear Regression process, move the variable selected to be the dependent variable from the left-hand window in the *Linear Regression* dialog box to the *Dependent* text box on the right-hand side of the *Linear Regression* dialog box. Then select the independent variables from the left-hand window in the *Linear Regression* dialog box and move them to the *Independent(s)* text box on the right-hand side of the *Linear Regression* dialog box. Next, click on the *Statistics* button to open the *Linear Regression: Statistics* dialog box. In the *Linear Regression: Statistics* dialog box assure that *Estimates* and *Model Fit* are checked and then click *Continue*.

Next click the *Options* button in the *Linear Regression* dialog box to open the *Linear Regression: Options* dialog box. In the *Linear Regression: Options* dialog box, assure that the *Include constant in equation* check box is checked. Next, click *Continue* in the *Linear Regression: Options* dialog box and then click the *OK* button in the *Linear Regression* dialog box.

The output of a Simple Linear Regression process follows.

```
REGRESSION
  /MISSING LISTWISE
  /STATISTICS COEFF OUTS R ANOVA
  /CRITERIA=PIN(.05) POUT(.10)
  /NOORIGIN
  /DEPENDENT profit
  /METHOD=ENTER nppp.
```

Regression

[DataSet1] C:\Documents and Settings\mill6391\Desktop\MyStuff\Research\Dissert
ation Data\MurrayScaledDissDataSPSS-8-9-2010.sav

Variables Entered/Removed[b]

Model	Variables Entered	Variables Removed	Method
1	nppp[a]	.	Enter

a. All requested variables entered.

b. Dependent Variable: profit

Model Summary

Model	R	R Square	Adjusted R Square	Std. Error of the Estimate
1	.383[a]	.147	.140	1.626

a. Predictors: (Constant), nppp

ANOVA[b]

Model		Sum of Squares	df	Mean Square	F	Sig.
1	Regression	56.486	1	56.486	21.378	.000[a]
	Residual	327.649	124	2.642		
	Total	384.135	125			

a. Predictors: (Constant), nppp

b. Dependent Variable: profit

Coefficients[a]

Model		Unstandardized Coefficients		Standardized Coefficients	t	Sig.
		B	Std. Error	Beta		
1	(Constant)	1.506	.497		3.029	.003
	nppp	.023	.005	.383	4.624	.000

a. Dependent Variable: profit

The following Excel screen shots, diagrams, and statistical outputs depict how a researcher can analyze data using *Simple Linear Regression*. The data pertaining to the variables of interest need to be situated on an Excel spreadsheet as noted in the following. Both variables portrayed in the following Excel spreadsheet represent the scaled variables to be analyzed. The two variables employed in this example are ***profit*** (perceived profit of a newly developed product) and ***nppp*** (overall new product development process proficiency). Therefore, the researcher is trying to determine how ***profit*** measured from a particular sample of firms is related to ***nppp***. The next screen shot depicts the variables of interest situated next to one another. Now, in the *Data Analysis* window, locate and click on *Regression* as noted below, and then click *OK*.

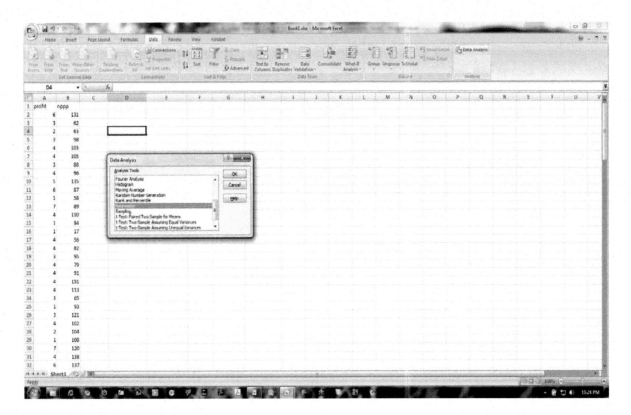

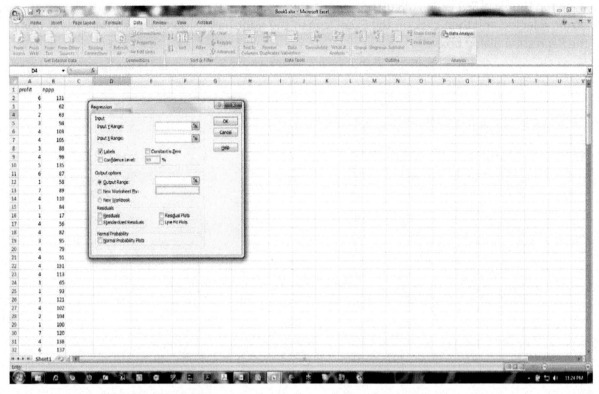

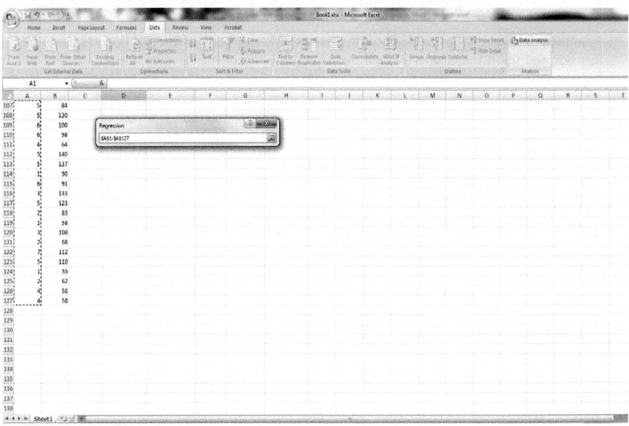

When the Excel *Regression* dialog box opens, the researcher needs to assure that the *Labels* check box is selected and then click on the Excel icon at the right-hand side of *Input Y Range* text box in the *Regression* dialog box.

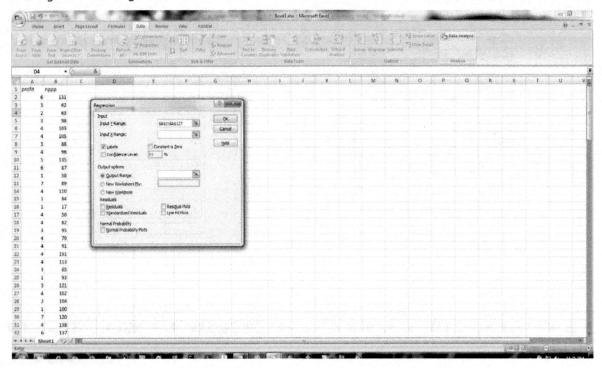

In the reduced *Regression* dialog box, the researcher should click on the right-hand side of the text box and select the column of data pertaining to profit or the selected dependent variable including the label or variable name in the first row.

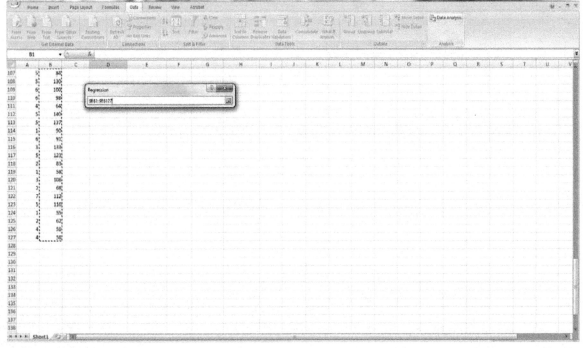

When the data is selected, the researcher needs to again click on the Excel icon on the right-hand side of the text box which now holds the range of the *Y* or dependent variable to return to the primary *Regression* dialog box. Then the researcher needs to click on the Excel icon at the right-hand side of *Input X Range* text box in the *Regression* dialog box.

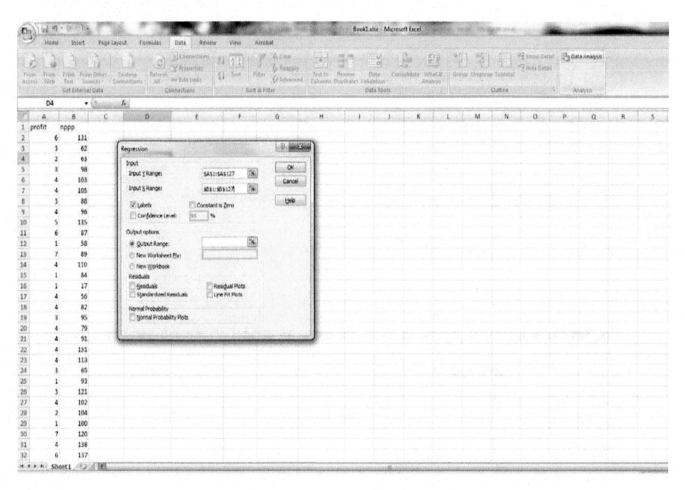

In the reduced *Regression* dialog box, the researcher should click on the right-hand side of the text box and select the column of data pertaining to **nppp**.

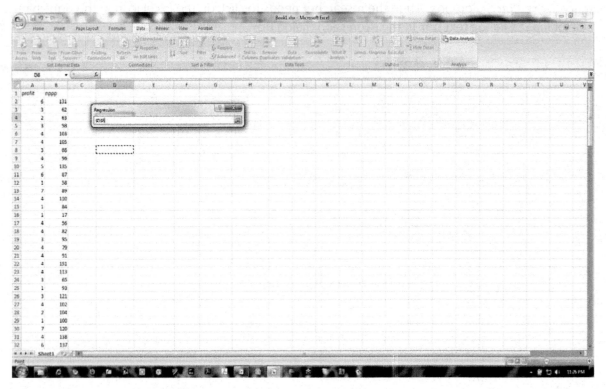

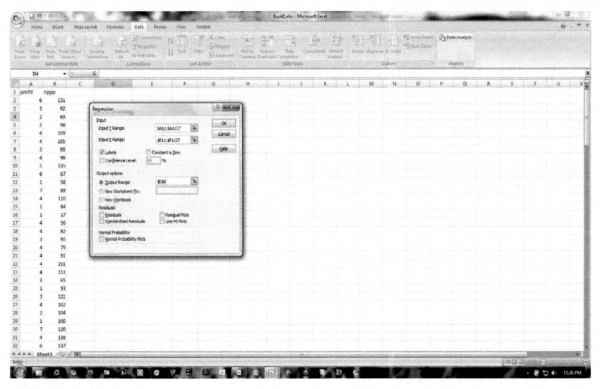

When the data is selected, the researcher needs to again click on the Excel icon on the right-hand side of the text box which now holds the range of the *X* or independent variable to return to the primary *Regression* dialog box. Next the researcher should assure that the *Output Range* radio button is selected.

Then the researcher should click on the Excel icon at the right-hand side of the *Output Range* text box to again open a reduced *Regression* text box. In this reduced *Regression* dialog box, the researcher needs to select the cell in which to place the upper left-hand corner of the *Simple Linear Regression* output. In this instance, the cell D8 is selected.

Next the researcher needs to click on the Excel icon at the right-hand side of the reduced *Regression* dialog box to return to the primary *Regression* dialog box.

To complete the *Simple Linear Regression* procedure and generate the output below, the researcher needs to click the **OK** button in the *Regression* dialog box.

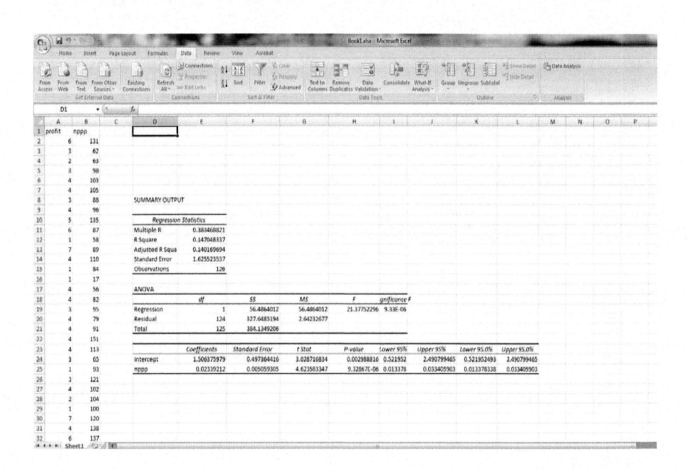

J. Multiple Regression

Multiple Regression is a process by which researchers can study several areas in which challenges can occur in Business and Marketing, and investigate questions that pertain to problems and opportunities that confront organizations. The first of two primary areas of inquiry for which *Multiple Regression* can be employed is *Predicting a value of a dependent variable* based on the information imbedded in several independent variables. A second important process that *Multiple Regression* can be used to perform is *simultaneously Comparing the relative influence* of several independent variables on a dependent variable. As will be noted in the following screen shots, the *Multiple Regression* process, when successfully performed, can result in equations based on empirical data that can be used as models of salient relationships.

Paragraphs K through M that follow the tutorial section below highlight additional important topics that relate to the successful implementation and execution of *Multiple Regression* processes.

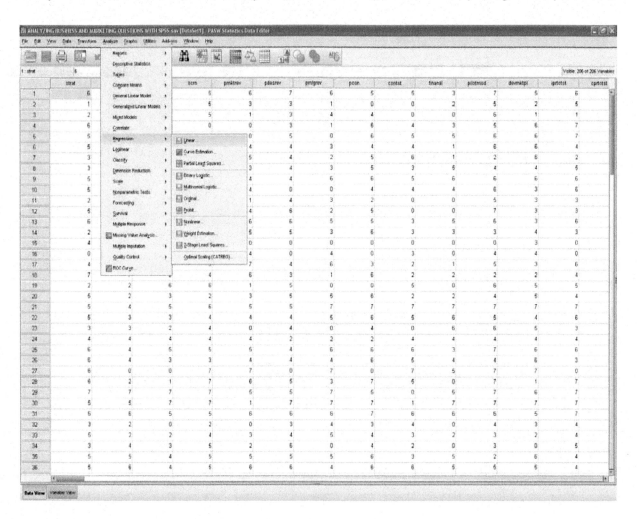

a. Examples and problems to be solved with Regression

- *Multiple Regression* can be used to provide researchers with statistical information that allow them to understand what form of Marketing communication is most important to customers who intend to purchase new products.
- *Multiple Regression* can also be used to provide researchers with empirically generated functions that can be used to predict the prices customers will pay for products based on a variety of independent factors which are significantly related to the price of selected products.
- *Multiple Regression* also allows researchers to test a variety of factors some of which, based on gathered empirical data, do not significantly influence a dependent variable of interest. For example, researchers might find that the degree to which survey respondents perceive the importance of the age of a firm does not have a significant impact on customers' satisfaction with their products.

The following SPSS screen shots, diagrams, and statistical outputs depict how a researcher can analyze data using Multiple Linear Regression and scaled (interval and/or ratio) data. To arrive at the SPSS screen shot below, click on *Analyze* on the menu bar and then click on *Regression* on the first drop-down menu and *Linear* on the second drop-down menu.

Next the researcher needs to move the selected dependent from the left-hand window in the *Linear Regression* dialog box to the *Dependent* text box on the right-hand side of the *Linear Regression* dialog box. When that step is completed, the researcher should move individually or together the independent variables from the left-hand window in the *Linear Regression* dialog box to the to the *Independent(s)* text box on the right-hand side of the *Regression* dialog box.

The researcher now needs to click on the *Statistics* button in the *Regression* dialog box. When the *Linear Regression: Statistics* dialog box opens, the researcher needs to assure that the *Estimates*, *Model fit*, and *Collinearity diagnostics* boxes are checked. When this is accomplished, the researcher can click the *Continue* button to return to the *Linear Regression* dialog box.

Now, in the *Linear Regression* dialog box the researcher should click on the *Options* button. In the *Linear Regression: Options* dialog box the researcher needs to assure that the *Include constant in equation* check box is filled. Then, the researcher should click Continue in the *Linear Regression: Options* dialog box and then OK in the *Linear Regression* dialog box to run the Multiple Regression procedure.

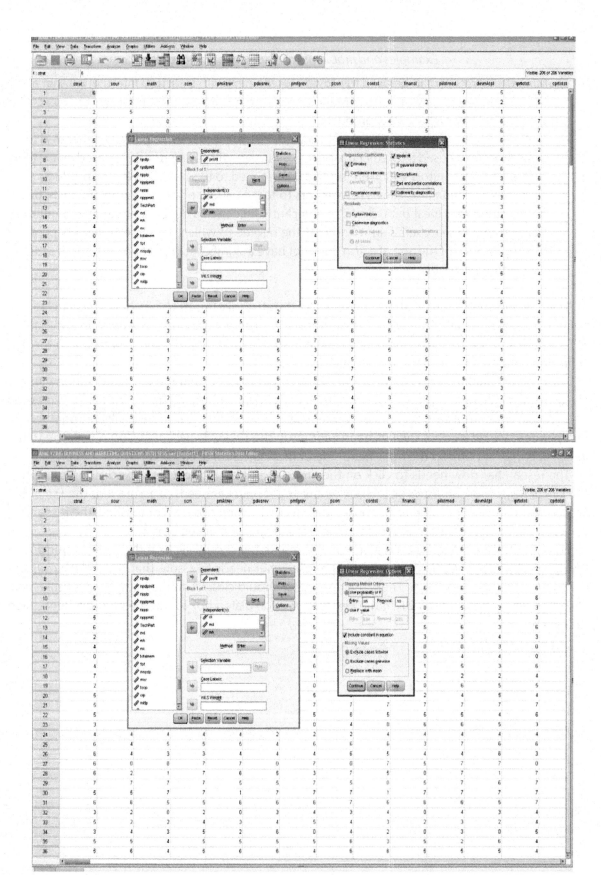

What follows is the output from the previously executed *Multiple Regression* process.

```
GET
  FILE='C:\Documents and Settings\mill6391\Desktop\MyStuff\Research\Dissertati
on Data\MurrayScaledDissDataSPSS-8-9-2010.sav'.
DATASET NAME DataSet1 WINDOW=FRONT.
REGRESSION
  /MISSING LISTWISE
  /STATISTICS COEFF OUTS R ANOVA COLLIN TOL
  /CRITERIA=PIN(.05) POUT(.10)
  /NOORIGIN
  /DEPENDENT profit
  /METHOD=ENTER nppp oi md mh.
```

Regression

```
[DataSet1] C:\Documents and Settings\mill6391\Desktop\MyStuff\Research\Dissert
ation Data\MurrayScaledDissDataSPSS-8-9-2010.sav
```

Variables Entered/Removed[b]

Model	Variables Entered	Variables Removed	Method
1	mh, oi, md, nppp[a]	.	Enter

a. All requested variables entered.

b. Dependent Variable: profit

Model Summary

Model	R	R Square	Adjusted R Square	Std. Error of the Estimate
1	.504[a]	.254	.228	1.540

a. Predictors: (Constant), mh, oi, md, nppp

ANOVA[b]

Model		Sum of Squares	df	Mean Square	F	Sig.
1	Regression	92.112	4	23.028	9.711	.000[a]
	Residual	270.325	114	2.371		
	Total	362.437	118			

a. Predictors: (Constant), mh, oi, md, nppp

b. Dependent Variable: profit

Coefficients[a]

Model		Unstandardized Coefficients		Standardized Coefficients	t	Sig.
		B	Std. Error	Beta		
1	(Constant)	1.022	.625		1.636	.105
	nppp	.015	.006	.255	2.582	.011
	oi	.013	.004	.325	3.405	.001
	md	-.052	.079	-.057	-.664	.508
	mh	-.089	.075	-.103	-1.179	.241

a. Dependent Variable: profit

Coefficients[a]

Model		Collinearity Statistics	
		Tolerance	VIF
1	(Constant)		
	nppp	.669	1.494
	oi	.718	1.393
	md	.882	1.133
	mh	.863	1.158

a. Dependent Variable: profit

Collinearity Diagnostics[a]

Model	Dimension	Eigenvalue	Condition Index	Variance Proportions		
				(Constant)	nppp	oi
1	1	4.606	1.000	.00	.00	.00
	2	.202	4.772	.01	.02	.05
	3	.114	6.354	.00	.02	.06
	4	.044	10.256	.46	.76	.04
	5	.034	11.600	.52	.20	.85

a. Dependent Variable: profit

Collinearity Diagnostics[a]

Model	Dimension	Variance Proportions	
		md	mh
1	1	.01	.01
	2	.78	.00
	3	.19	.84
	4	.00	.01
	5	.02	.14

a. Dependent Variable: profit

The following Excel screen shots, diagrams, and statistical outputs depict how a researcher can analyze data using *Multiple Linear Regression*. The same Excel Regression entry point is used that was employed to initiate the *Simple Linear Regression* process.

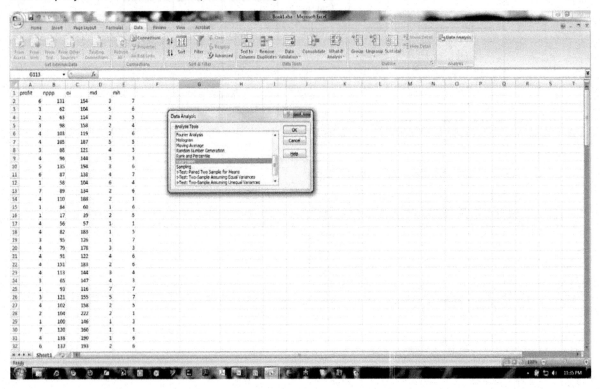

The data pertaining to the variables of interest need to be situated on an Excel spreadsheet as noted in the following screen shot. In this case, five variables are depicted in the following Excel spreadsheet and represent the one dependent and four independent scaled variables to be analyzed. The one dependent variable employed in this example is **profit** (perceived profit of a newly developed product). The four independent variables are **nppp** (overall new product development process proficiency), **oi** (degree of overall organizational integration which indicates how well product development groups internal and external to a firm cooperate), **md** (degree of market dynamism or customer volatility as perceived by new product development managers), and **mh** (degree of market hostility or market competitiveness as perceived by new product development managers). Therefore, the researcher is trying to determine how **profit** measured from a particular sample of firms is related to **nppp**, **oi**, **md**, and **mh**. The next, screen shot depicts the variables of interest situated next to one another. Now, in the *Data Analysis* window, locate and click on *Regression*, as noted below, and then click *OK*.

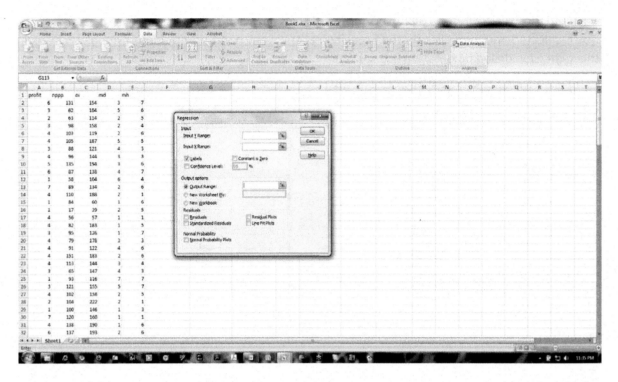

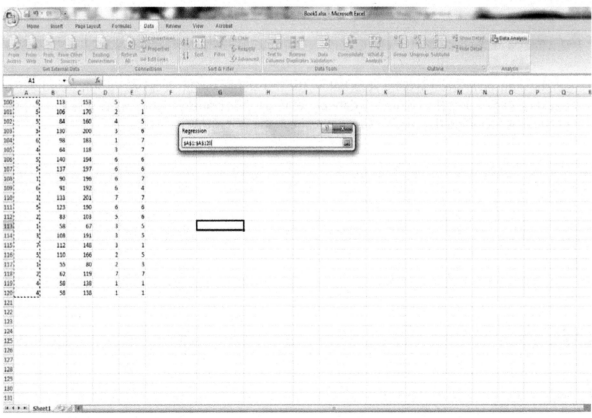

When the Excel *Regression* dialog box opens, the researcher needs to assure that the *Labels* check box is selected and then click on the Excel icon at the right-hand side of *Input Y Range* text box in the *Regression* dialog box.

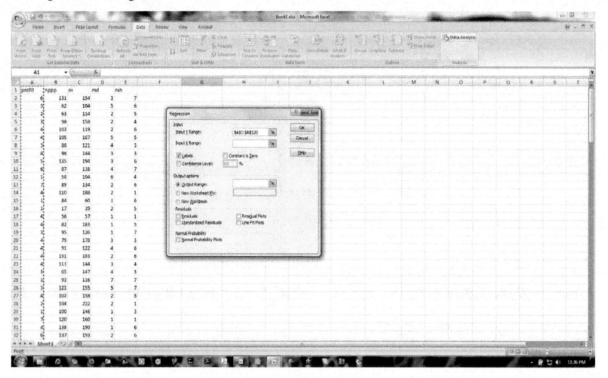

In the reduced *Regression* dialog box below, the researcher should click on the right-hand side of the text box and select the column of data pertaining to the **profit** variable or the selected dependent variable including the label or variable name in the first row.

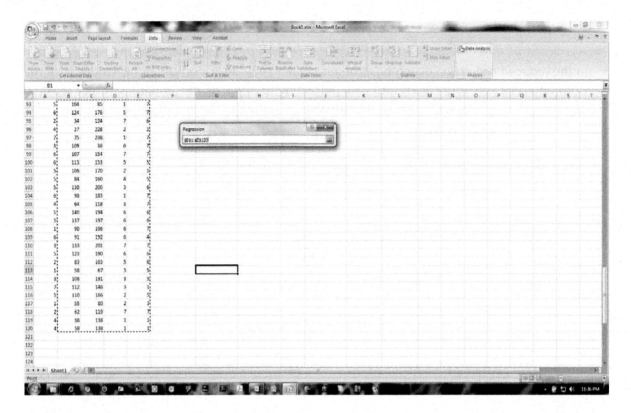

After the dependent variable data is selected, the researcher needs to again click on the Excel icon on the right-hand side of the text box which now holds the range of the *Y* or dependent variable to return to the primary *Regression* dialog box. Then, the researcher needs to click on the Excel icon at the right-hand side of *Input X Range* text box in the *Regression* dialog box.

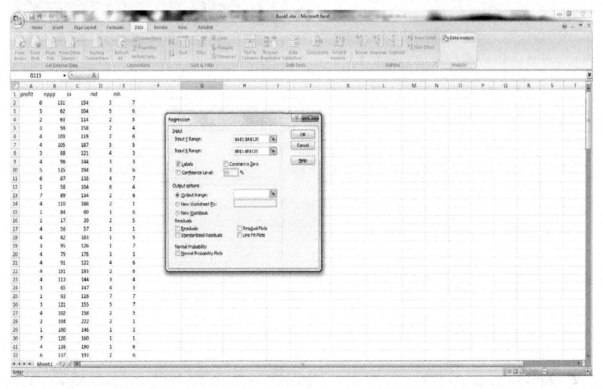

In the reduced *Regression* dialog box, the researcher should click on the right-hand side of the text box and select the four columns of data pertaining to **nppp**, **oi**, **md**, and **mh** or other selected independent variables including their labels or variable names in the first row.

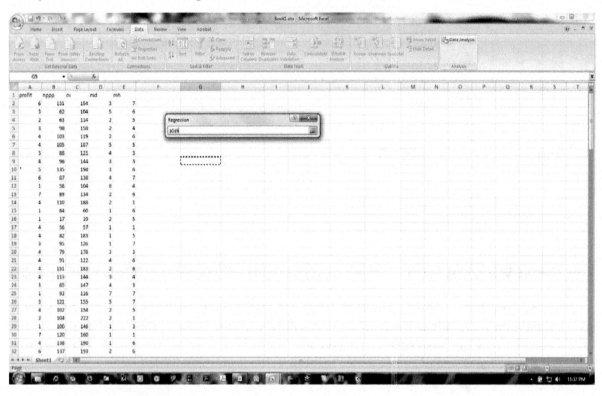

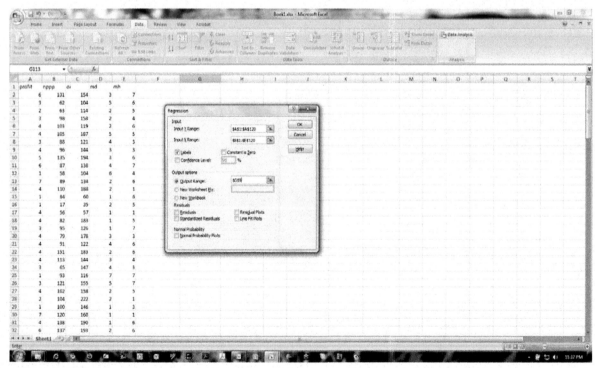

When the data is selected, the researcher needs to again click on the Excel icon on the right-hand side of the text box which now holds the range of the *X* or independent variables to return to the primary *Regression* dialog box. Next the researcher should assure that the *Output Range* radio button is selected.

Then the researcher should click on the Excel icon at the right-hand side of the *Output Range* text box to again open a reduced *Regression* text box. In this reduced *Regression* dialog box, the researcher needs to select the cell in which to place the upper left-hand corner of the *Multiple Linear Regression* output. In this instance, the cell G9 is selected.

Next the researcher needs to click on the Excel icon at the right-hand side of the reduced *Regression* dialog box to return to the primary *Regression* dialog box.

To complete the *Multiple Linear Regression* procedure and generate the output below, the researcher needs to click the **OK** button in the *Regression* dialog box.

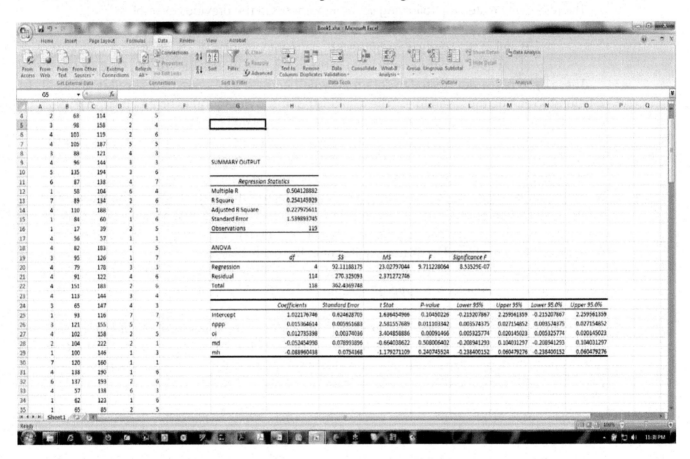

Findings Using Regression:

In this instance, the researcher is trying to determine whether there is a relationship between **profit**, which is a scaled, dependent variable that represents the perceived profit of the new products under investigation in this sample, and four independent variables that include **nppp**, which represents the overall proficiency with which a new product development process is performed, **oi**, which represents the overall degree of integration among organizational groups to facilitate the development of new products, **md**, which represents market dynamism or the degree of changes in the marketplace associated with customers desire for the new products under consideration, and **mh**, which represents market hostility or the degree of competitiveness in the marketplace regarding the new products being studied. All of these variables were measured using 7 point, interval scales. It is therefore appropriate for the researcher to use the Regression process to determine the possible influence of these four variables on perceived profit.

The researcher tested the following set of hypotheses in the previous examples.

H_0: All of the coefficients of the independent variables $(\beta_1, \beta_2, \beta_3, \beta_4) = 0$

H_A: At least one the coefficients of the independent variables $(\beta_1, \beta_2, \beta_3, \beta_4) \neq 0$

These hypotheses were tested to determine whether there is an overall statistically significant relationship among these variables. The resulting F statistic was found to be 9.711 with a **p** value of 0.000. This suggests that the researcher should reject the null hypothesis.

The researcher should employ an $\alpha = 0.05$ unless there is a compelling reason to use another value.

Now that the overall model appears to be significant, the researcher needs to investigate the four independent variable coefficients to determine which of the coefficients are significant. The multiple regression output notes that **nppp** (**p** = 0.011) and **oi** (**p** = 0.001) have **p** values that are below 0.05 which suggests their significance to the researcher. The **md** (**p** = 0.508) and **mh** (**p** = 0.241) variables were found to be not significant at the $\alpha = 0.05$ level.

The researcher also needs to note the standardized coefficients. The standardized coefficients for the significant variables are **nppp** (**β** = 0.255) and **oi** (**β** = 0.325). It should also be noted that both of these betas are positive.

The analysis of *Simple Regression* projects is the same as the analysis of *Multiple Regression* projects however with regard to *Simple Regression* projects there is no need to review the coefficients since there only exists a single independent variable and if that variable was insignificant, the entire regression would also be insignificant.

Implications of Research Using Regression:

The researcher should learn from this test that the model is significant which means that the variables that were selected for the model are related to one another and specifically that the independent variables have a significant influence on the dependent variable.

Next the researcher should note that two of the four independent variables tested were found to be significantly related to the dependent variable. If predictions were to be made, the two insignificant variables should be removed from the model and the regression rerun to arrive at the appropriate beta coefficient values. The two significant independent variables included **nppp** (overall new product process proficiency) and **oi** (overall organizational integration). A comparison of the two significant standardized, beta coefficients informs the researcher that the **oi** standardized beta coefficient is larger than the **nppp** standardized beta coefficient. This observation tells the researcher that the degree of organizational integration related to the development of new products has a greater impact on the perceived profits associated with new products' success than the overall proficiency with which new products are developed.

K. Making Predictions with Regression and Comparing Independent Variable Coefficients

Regression models are used for two primary purposes that include making predictions of the *Y* variable under various conditions and determining the relative impact of various independent variables. When *Regression* models are used to compare the relative influence of independent variable coefficients, the Coefficient of Determination is not as important as it is when the use of a *Regression* model is prediction. When prediction is the objective, the Coefficient of Determination needs to be large, since a significant percent of the variance in the dependent variable needs to be explained simultaneously by all of the independent variables in the model.

When the purpose of investigating a Regression model is to determine the relative influence of various independent variables, the magnitude of the standardized variable coefficients or standardized (βs) need to be compared. Using standardized coefficients eliminates the impact of variables that are measured using non-comparable metrics. In these instances, the larger the β, the greater the influence a particular *X* variable has on the *Y* variable regardless of the sign of the coefficient. The sign of the coefficient determines whether the influence is a direct influence (plus sign) or an inverse influence (minus sign).

L. Dummy Variables

The process of incorporating *Dummy Variables* in a Regression model is technique for including nominal/categorical variables in a Regression model. A two-category nominal data variable can easily be incorporated into a Regression model. The two categories need to be coded 0 and 1 to facilitate the Dummy Variable's inclusion. The effect of Dummy Variables on the slopes of Regression model graphs is that the Dummy Variables create parallel lines with the same slope as the X_1 variable which is described below. The following portrays in equation form how a Dummy Variable can be inserted into a Regression equation.

$Y = \beta_0 + \beta_1 X_1 + \beta_2 X_2 + \varepsilon$ where β_0 is the constant term or intercept of the *Y* axis; β_1 and β_2 are independent variable coefficients of X_1 and X_2; and ε is an error term.

Assume that X_2 is a Dummy Variable with data coded 0 and 1. In the equation above, when X_2 is equal to 0, the equation is as follows.

$$Y = \beta_0 + \beta_1 X_1 + \varepsilon$$

However, when X_2 equals 1, the equation can be depicted as follows.

$$Y = (\beta_0 + \beta_2) + \beta_1 X_1 + \varepsilon$$

As noted above, the slope is β_1 which is the same as the slope of the X_1 variable. Moreover, when X_1 is 0, the Y intercept is β_0. However, when X_1 is 1, the Y intercept increases or decreases, if β_2 is negative, to $(\beta_0 + \beta_2)$ which demonstrates that the two lines are parallel. Dummy variables can be represented by more than two categories such as the colors Red, Blue, and Green. In the example described above, the number of variables in the equation is 1 which results from evaluating $k - 1$ where k is the total number of categories of the nominal variable which is 2 in this case. If the number of categories were 3 such as in the example regarding the colors Red, Blue, and Green, the number of variables would be 2 or $k - 1$ where k is equal to 3.

M. Multicollinearity-Variance Inflation Factor

Multicollinearity describes the correlation that can occur between independent variables in a *Regression* model. When multicollinearity is present, several unwanted effects can occur such as the following.

- When a variable is added to a Regression model, the estimate of the standard deviation of the Regression model error can increase.
- When a variable is added to a Regression model, a significantly large change in the model's coefficients can occur.
- The addition of a variable to a Regression model may change the signs of the model's coefficients.
- When a variable is added to a Regression model, a variable that was significant may become insignificant.

Researchers should calculate the correlations among all independent variables to assess the magnitude of the correlation coefficients. Additionally, the Variance Inflation Factors (VIF) should be calculated for all independent variables. A VIF of 1.0 indicates that there is no multicollinearity. A rule of thumb for eliminating an independent variable from the Regression model is noting a VIF of 10.0. A more conservative measure that is also used is a VIF of 5.0. The equation for determining a VIF for each independent variable follows.

VIF = $1 / (1 - R_j^2)$ where R_j^2 is the Coefficient of Determination that results when the jth independent variable is regressed against the remaining $k - 1$ variables.

N. Scope of a Model

The scope of a *Regression* model needs to be bounded by the data that were used to create the model. This suggests that the range of the independent variables acts as the extremities, boundaries, or scope of a *Regression* model.

For example, a researcher wants to develop a *Regression* model to predict the impact of business factors on new product success. Assume a *Regression* model that comprises two independent variables and a single dependent variable. A sample of 200 firms was surveyed to gather data regarding a single dependent variable which is new product revenue and two independent variables that comprise the number of employees applied to the development of a new product and the direct investment in R&D equipment that was used to develop a new product. Also, assume that the range of employees developing new products for the firms in the sample was 4 on the low end and 12 on the high end, whereas the range of direct investment in R&D equipment for the development of the new products in the sample was $12,000 on the low end and $25,000 on the high end. Now assume that the first year new product revenue generated relative to the new products in the sample was $45,000 on the low end and $103,000 on the high end. The data obtained from the 200 firms were employed to create a predictive *Regression* model so that when values for the number of employees developing new products and the direct investment in R&D equipment for the development of a new product are entered into the equation resulting from this research, an estimate of first-year new product revenue can be obtained.

The scope of the values for which this *Regression* model is expected to be valid and useful is bound by the range of new product developing employees between 4 and 12 and a direct R&D equipment investment of $45,000 to $103,000. If it is necessary to include a number of new product developing employees that is less than 4 or greater than 12, or direct R&D equipment investment that is less than $45,000 or greater than $103,000, the *Regression* model discussed here may not provide valid results because the actual relationships among these variables in the population/environment may not behave in the manner described by this *Regression* model.

O. References

http://www.purplemath.com/modules/scattreg.htm
http://www.ltcconline.net/greenl/courses/201/regression/scatter.htm
http://mallit.fr.umn.edu/fr4218/assigns/excel_reg.html

Appendix

Table 1. Percentage Points of the T-Distribution

α–One Tail	0.10	0.05	0.025	0.01	0.005	0.001	0.0005	α–One Tail
α–Two Tails	0.20	0.10	0.05	0.02	0.01	0.002	0.001	α–Two Tails
d.f.= 1	3.078	6.314	12.71	31.82	63.66	318.3	637	d.f.= 1
d.f.=2	1.886	2.920	4.303	6.965	9.925	22.33	31.6	d.f.=2
d.f.=3	1.638	2.353	3.182	4.541	5.841	10.210	12.92	d.f.=3
d.f.=4	1.533	2.132	2.776	3.747	4.604	7.173	8.610	d.f.=4
d.f.=5	1.476	2.015	2.571	3.365	4.032	5.893	6.869	d.f.=5
d.f.=6	1.440	1.943	2.447	3.143	3.707	5.208	5.959	d.f.=6
d.f.=7	1.415	1.895	2.365	2.998	3.499	4.785	5.408	d.f.=7
d.f.=8	1.397	1.860	2.306	2.896	3.355	4.501	5.041	d.f.=8
d.f.=9	1.383	1.833	2.262	2.821	3.250	4.297	4.781	d.f.=9
d.f.=10	1.372	1.812	2.228	2.764	3.169	4.144	4.587	d.f.=10
d.f.=11	1.363	1.796	2.201	2.718	3.106	4.025	4.437	d.f.=11
d.f.=12	1.356	1.782	2.179	2.681	3.055	3.930	4.318	d.f.=12
d.f.=13	1.350	1.771	2.160	2.650	3.012	3.852	4.221	d.f.=13
d.f.=14	1.345	1.761	2.145	2.624	2.977	3.787	4.140	d.f.=14
d.f.=15	1.341	1.753	2.131	2.602	2.947	3.733	4.073	d.f.=15
d.f.=16	1.337	1.746	2.120	2.583	2.921	3.686	4.015	d.f.=16
d.f.=17	1.333	1.740	2.110	2.567	2.898	3.646	3.965	d.f.=17
d.f.=18	1.330	1.734	2.101	2.552	2.878	3.610	3.922	d.f.=18
d.f.=19	1.328	1.729	2.093	2.539	2.861	3.579	3.883	d.f.=19
d.f.=20	1.325	1.725	2.086	2.528	2.845	3.552	3.850	d.f.=20
d.f.=21	1.323	1.721	2.080	2.518	2.831	3.527	3.819	d.f.=21
d.f.=22	1.321	1.717	2.074	2.508	2.819	3.505	3.792	d.f.=22
d.f.=23	1.319	1.714	2.069	2.500	2.807	3.485	3.768	d.f.=23
d.f.=24	1.318	1.711	2.064	2.492	2.797	3.467	3.745	d.f.=24
d.f.=25	1.316	1.708	2.060	2.485	2.787	3.450	3.725	d.f.=25
d.f.=26	1.315	1.706	2.056	2.479	2.779	3.435	3.707	d.f.=26
d.f.=27	1.314	1.703	2.052	2.473	2.771	3.421	3.690	d.f.=27
d.f.=28	1.313	1.701	2.048	2.467	2.763	3.408	3.674	d.f.=28
d.f.=29	1.311	1.699	2.045	2.462	2.756	3.396	3.659	d.f.=29
d.f.=30	1.310	1.697	2.042	2.457	2.750	3.385	3.646	d.f.=30
d.f.=32	1.309	1.694	2.037	2.449	2.738	3.365	3.622	d.f.=32
d.f.=34	1.307	1.691	2.032	2.441	2.728	3.348	3.601	d.f.=34
d.f.=36	1.306	1.688	2.028	2.434	2.719	3.333	3.582	d.f.=36
d.f.=38	1.304	1.686	2.024	2.429	2.712	3.319	3.566	d.f.=38
d.f.=40	1.303	1.684	2.021	2.423	2.704	3.307	3.551	d.f.=40
d.f.=42	1.302	1.682	2.018	2.418	2.698	3.296	3.538	d.f.=42
d.f.=44	1.301	1.680	2.015	2.414	2.692	3.286	3.526	d.f.=44
d.f.=46	1.300	1.679	2.013	2.410	2.687	3.277	3.515	d.f.=46
d.f.=48	1.299	1.677	2.011	2.407	2.682	3.269	3.505	d.f.=48
d.f.=50	1.299	1.676	2.009	2.403	2.678	3.261	3.496	d.f.=50
d.f.=55	1.297	1.673	2.004	2.396	2.668	3.245	3.476	d.f.=55
d.f.=60	1.296	1.671	2.000	2.390	2.660	3.232	3.460	d.f.=60
d.f.=65	1.295	1.669	1.997	2.385	2.654	3.220	3.447	d.f.=65
d.f.=70	1.294	1.667	1.994	2.381	2.648	3.211	3.435	d.f.=70
d.f.=80	1.292	1.664	1.990	2.374	2.639	3.195	3.416	d.f.=80
d.f.=100	1.290	1.660	1.984	2.364	2.626	3.174	3.390	d.f.=100
d.f.=150	1.287	1.655	1.976	2.351	2.609	3.145	3.357	d.f.=150
d.f.=200	1.286	1.653	1.972	2.345	2.601	3.131	3.340	d.f.=200
Two Tails	0.20	0.10	0.05	0.02	0.01	0.002	0.001	Two Tails
One Tail	0.10	0.05	0.025	0.01	0.005	0.001	0.0005	One Tail

Retrieved from http://www.siliconfareast.com/t-dist.htm, December 30, 2010.

CPSIA information can be obtained
at www.ICGtesting.com
Printed in the USA
LVOW04*2246170817
545411LV00008BA/13/P